D1420329

A
YEAR
IN
REFLECTION

Pictures and thoughts by Fr. James Mc Sweeney

Thomas Crosbie Holdings Limited

Evening Echo

Published 2007
By Echo Publications (Cork) Limited
City Quarter, Lapps Quay, Cork.
A Thomas Crosbie Holdings Company

ISBN: 978-0-9528856-7-2

Design and layout by Damien Callender
Printed by Walsh Colour Print

DEDICATION

I dedicate this book to my parents Con and Nora who have guided me through my life and are always an inspiration in everything I do.

Buíochas

This book 'A Year In Reflection' would not have become a reality without Diarmuid O'Donovan, Circulation Manager of the Evening Echo. He gently steered this book from an idea into reality.

Particular thanks to Damien Callender who designed and laid out the book. His expertise is evident on every page and he has made the book so easy to read.

Thanks to the Evening Echo team of Orla Keane, Lisa O'Connor, Eoghan Dinan, Deirdre O'Reilly, Stephen Dinan, Rory Noonan, Kevin Smith, Mary White, Louise O'Flynn, Kieran Dineen, Maurice Gubbins, Dan Linehan and especially Brian Lougheed, for their input and support in putting this book together.

A particular mention for my parents, Con and Nora, my sisters Teresa and Kathryn, my brothers Denis and Gerard, my nephews Daniel and Peter and my niece Aoife for their love and support over the years.

Thanks to Bishop John Buckley, the Blackpool team of Fr John O'Donovan PP and Fr Christy Harrington for their support and encouragement.

A final thank you to all my friends and particularly the parish team and people of Ballyvolane / Dublin Hill for making me feel so at home in the parish.

If I have forgotten anyone, I apologise sincerely.

FOREWORD

'The privilege of a lifetime is being who you are.'
~Joseph Campbell

Putting together 'A Year In Reflection' has been a great privilege for me.
I count myself so lucky and honoured to get the chance to share some of my photography and thoughts in this book. The photographs cover every aspect of life, from nature, wildlife, sport, to the human side of life. It has been said that photography is a way of feeling, of touching and loving. What is caught on camera is captured forever. It remembers the little things, long after we have forgotten everything. This book is a collection of many little things. Every photo has been selected to uplift, encourage and inspire. Each photo has featured on my website www.todayismygifttoyou.ie or has been printed in the Evening Echo.

The short thoughts under each photograph are also gentle but meaningful. These thoughts have also featured on the website and are printed each day in the Evening Echo. They have their roots firmly intertwined with every aspect of life, love and faith. They have been inspired by you but most importantly they have been inspired by a loving God.

This book gives you the opportunity to pick it up each day. As we journey through the year there is a space for you to add in your own personal information like birthdays, anniversaries etc. Most importantly enjoy the book. Don't read it all through in one go!! One step and one day at a time is always the best way to go.

Thanks to the Evening Echo for the chance to share this book with you. They have nurtured, supported and encouraged my interest in photography. I will be forever grateful.

James McSweeney

JANUARY

Fireworks at Lourdes, France

JANUARY 1ST

'We spend the early days of January walking through our lives, room by room, drawing up a list of work to be done, cracks to be patched. Maybe this year, to balance the list, we ought to walk through the rooms of our lives…not looking for flaws but for potential.'
~Ellen Goodman

New Year's resolutions all evolve around correcting what's negative. It's little wonder that they don't last. Of course it's important to check in on what needs improving but so often we concentrate only on the negative. As we begin this New Year why not check in on all that's good and positive in our lives. This is a great starting point. We can use all that's good and positive as areas of growth and potential. When this happens the negative begins to be squeezed out. The message of the gospels reminds us that it won't all happen today, but most certainly will over time.

NOTES:

Snowfall at Tooreenbawn, Millstreet, Co.Cork

JANUARY 2ND

'We will open the book. Its pages are blank. We are going to put words on them ourselves. This book is called opportunity and its first chapter is the first week of the New Year.'
~Edith Pierce

The start of the New Year is always greeted with enthusiasm. There is a sense of beginning a new journey, leaving old and worn roads behind us, making positive changes in our lives and looking forward in hope.

We won't be able to change the world, we won't be able to do a complete changeover, but we can be open to trying some small positive changes in our lives. Every day presents new opportunities but especially the start of a new year. We welcome these opportunities and for us to know that God is gently journeying with us in all our hopes, dreams and plans for this New Year.

 NOTES

Daniel McSweeney making the most of lunchtime

JANUARY 3RD

'It is the tragedy of the world that no one knows what they don't know and the less a person knows, the more sure they are that they know everything.'
~Joyce Cary

There is nothing worse than someone who thinks they know everything. This leads to complacency, pride, and superiority. Very few can really say they know everything but many can say they have learned from life's many experiences. It's not about how much we know that matters but much more about being open to learning about life and ourselves. The start of a new year is an ideal time to be open to something fresh and new in our lives. In our Gospels Jesus gently moved people from what was old and stale to something totally new and energising. The same invitation is also extended to us. Knowing everything isn't always important but much more important is knowing that now is the moment.

 NOTES:

A squirrel in Central Park, New York

JANUARY 4TH

'A small boy watched his elder brother jump out of his car, run round to the other side and open the door for his girlfriend. The young boy turned sadly to his friend and said, "Jack always has to do that. She's beautiful but she's not very strong!"

It just goes to show that what we do can be interpreted in lots of different ways especially in the eyes of a child. Even a simple act of kindness can be picked up in different ways. Every action of ours, good and bad, always has a knock on effect. As we start the New Year it is good for us to try and put the emphasis more on what's good and positive. Others may choose differently but we can choose wisely. The knock on effects are always good, encouraging and the best way of living the values of the Gospel.

 NOTES

Winter sunset at Tooreenbawn, Millstreet, Co.Cork

JANUARY 5TH

'We have the greatest pre-nuptial agreement in the world. It's called love.'
~Gene Perret

One of God's greatest gifts to us is love, not just romantic love but all types of love that bring energy and life to our daily routines. Sometimes love in our lives lacks energy and direction. Left unchecked it can stagnate and even die. Everyone may be getting back into a normal routine again after the Christmas. It is easy to let the message of Christmas behind us as we move on with our lives. At the heart of the message of Christmas is God's deep and unique love for us. These days of January are an opportune time to rekindle those sparks of love that bring life and energy into our lives. Anything taken for granted is bound to get stuck including love. It is up to us to make sure love always brings life and energy.

NOTES:

A Year in Reflection

Stained Glass of Epiphany at Pau, France

JANUARY 6TH

'Then opening their treasures, they offered him gifts of gold, frankincense and myrrh.'
~Matthew 2:11

You'd have to feel sorry for the wise men. Just when most people are taking down Christmas trees and decorations, the wise men arrive when everyone else is finishing up. But the feast of the Epiphany, which we celebrate today, is an important one. Just like the wise men we are also searching for meaning and purpose to life. We are looking for answers to our deepest questions. The journey of the wise men reminds us that those who are searching for something deeper will find God in their lives. God is waiting to be discovered in the places and people that we least expect God to be. We pray today for guidance and direction in our own daily journey. Like the wise men we also pray for strength and courage on our journey especially when it's easier to quit.

✒ NOTES

Frosty Leaf at Myross Wood Retreat House, Leap, West Cork

JANUARY 7TH

'I've started so I'll finish'
~Magnus Magnusson

The quiz programme Mastermind has enthralled millions of viewers down through the years. For years Magnus Magnusson coined the catchphrase that everyone knew and loved, "I've started so I'll finish." Those are wise words for us too and in particular for how we approach life. It is always great to start a job at hand but much better to finish it well. Too big a task or too many together never works. The call of the gospel is to work with what God has given to us and to use our own specific gifts and talents to help us choose what we can do. The finishing line may sometimes seem a long distance away but God always helps us cross that finishing line come what may.

NOTES:

Young calf on the Buckley Farm, Ballinahina, Co. Cork

JANUARY 8TH

'Life's battles don't always go to the stronger or fastest person.
But sooner or later, the person who wins is the one who thinks they can.'
~Author Unknown

Every single one of us faces those ongoing life battles. Even with a new year these battles still go on. Life is fragile and its sharp edges touch everyone at some stage. We sometimes think that others have the edge on us but they don't really. If we think we are beaten in life then we most certainly are. But if we are willing to face everything with some courage and determination we will pull through. Equally we may have to reach out and help somebody else who thinks they are beaten. It can so easily happen with a lack of self confidence, a bout of depression or just being overwhelmed by what lies ahead. We can be the one who can gently give them the confidence to take that all important step forward.

 NOTES

January snowdrop on the Cashman Farm, Tullig, Millstreet, Co. Cork

JANUARY 9TH

'There were six stone water jars; each could hold 20 or 30 gallons. The steward tasted the water and it had turned into wine.'
~extract from the story of the wedding feast of Cana

There are many angles to this story, but one is that Jesus is talking about the shortages in each of our own lives. Has love dried up in our relationships? Are we bored with life and settling for humdrum routine? Have we tossed aside our hopes, dreams and plans? Are we run down and tired of life and living? Jesus is calling us to change and to welcome new beginnings. It doesn't just happen for the first few days of January, it happens today and throughout the coming week. It is never too late to start. Jesus changed the water into wine. If we want to change we also must turn to Jesus, because wherever Jesus is found, life is always changed for the better.

 NOTES:

A Year in Reflection

Red buds at Charlie Wilkin's garden, Mayfield, Cork

JANUARY 10TH

'January can be a revealing month with gardens pared down to their bones. The sun is clean and low and this side-lighting will always pick out forms and shapes that in summer are flattened by bright overhead light.'
~Charlie Wilkins

A bright light is useful but does have its limitations. We all know people who are dominant, harsh, bullish and loud. They may not even realise just how ineffective their harsh bright light is. But we can be such effective side-lighting. Using words of encouragement and praise, words of thanks and support or words of appreciation and kindness, can make all the difference. This is side-lighting at its best. In our Gospels Jesus often worked from the side. He took people in need of help away from the glare of the crowd and gave them his undivided attention. Working gently and quietly from the side, gives the space to be a real friend to someone.

 NOTES

Sunrise on Mushera Mountain near Millstreet, Co.Cork

JANUARY 11TH

'Deal with the faults of others as gently as your own.'
~Chinese Proverb

An eagle has got incredible eyesight, far better than the human eye. From amazing heights it can spot the tiniest of movement at ground level. Like an eagle we are so quick to see, but in our case we often just zoom in on the faults of others. Faults seem to overshadow and crowd out all our good and positive qualities. Like many faults some are repairable and some are so in built that nothing can change them. We sometimes are very hard on other people's faults. Equally we are all slow to admit or even realise that we too have faults. Dealing with the faults of others as gently as our own, will ensure that we will not be as hard in picking on the faults of others.

 NOTES:

A Year in Reflection

Gate of snow at Tooreenbawn, Millstreet, Co.Cork

JANUARY 12TH

'Middle age is when your narrow waist and broad mind begin to change places.'
~Author Unknown

Whatever about middle age, January is a month when everyone is aware of their waist line. Gyms and walkways are so busy during this month. Exercise is always important but an equally important exercise is keeping an open and broad mind on all aspects of life. As we grow older we can never say we have done everything or have it all worked out. The best example of someone with a broad mind is to be found in our Gospels. Jesus gently and sensitively dealt with each person knowing that life's many unfolding events are experienced differently by every person. If we can keep an open mind with all aspects of living, then we are in the best position to grow and adapt to the challenges and joys of every day.

NOTES

A Ford Ka car becomes a unique fish aquarium at Amsterdam

JANUARY 13TH

'If you want to catch more fish, use more hooks.'
~George Allen

Fish are funny creatures. They are always so busy and at times busy for the sake of being busy. They are always on the move, they flirt about, dashing here and there, full of enthusiasm and watching everything. They are so easily alarmed by every ripple, so ready for the unexpected and yet so easily caught too. There is a certain 'fishiness' about us too. Like fish we are immersed in a sea of troubles and distractions. Like fish we are easily alarmed, we often waste energy on what's trivial and we play with temptations. It is so easy to allow ourselves to be hooked on what we think brings satisfaction and happiness. What areas of my life need to be unhooked? Can I let go of unnecessary anger and guilt? Can I let go of hurts and mistakes made? Can I replace any of my unhooking with a sense of God's great love for me?

NOTES:

Angry heron at Fota Gardens, near Cobh, Co.Cork

JANUARY 14TH

'Words are only postage stamps delivering the object for you to unwrap.'
~George Bernard Shaw

The 6 most important words: "I admit I made a mistake."
The 5 most important words: "You did a good job."
The 4 most important words: "What is your opinion?"
The 3 most important words: "I love you."
The 2 most important words: "Thank you."
The 1 most important word: "We"
The least important word: "I"

To sum all this up from God's point of view, means we are loved by God, we are human and open to making mistakes, we thank God for all our blessings, we work best not on our own but together and as a part of God's family we can accomplish much together.

 NOTES

Curly branches at Tooreenbawn, Millstreet, Co.Cork

JANUARY 15TH

'To be good instruments of God's love we must avoid being over tired, burnt out, stressed, aggressive, dispersed or closed up. We need to be rested, centred, peaceful and aware of the needs of our body, our heart and our spirit.'
~Jean Vanier

When we are tired and wearied it is hard to do anything. It is even more difficult on a spiritual level, to do anything proper. The invitation each day is to share God's love with other people but only if we ourselves are relaxed and rested. It is always a difficult challenge to find the balance between work, rest and play. Finding this balance was nearly impossible last month such was the hectic pace of life. But as we journey through this month of January, there is a much better chance of finding it. We can make a start today. Are we going to create some quiet time for ourselves now or later?

 NOTES:

A Year in Reflection

Early flower in January at Charlie Wilkin's garden, Mayfield, Cork

JANUARY 16TH

'Every day cannot be a feast of lanterns.'
~Chinese Proverb

We sometimes may feel that life is boring and that everything is too predictable and routine. Maybe different aspects of our lives that were full of energy, now feel as if they're gone stale. We begin to whisper to ourselves, "I'm missing something", "There's more to life than this." So we begin to push the boundaries out and this can be a very good thing to do. But sometimes we begin to push out unhealthy boundaries. To compensate for boredom we try and have it all. But life doesn't work like that and if it does, it catches up on us very quickly. No one can ever have it all and that's why routine is never an enemy. It may not always be good looking or attractive but at least it brings some stability into our lives. The moment we're restless and feel that we're missing out, is always a good time to take stock and just realise how lucky we actually are.

✎ NOTES

A Year in Reflection 16

Drishane Castle, Millstreet, Co.Cork, silhouetted in the evening sunlight

JANUARY 17TH

'I used to think that God's gifts were on shelves, one above the other and the taller we grow the easier we can reach them. Now I find that God's gifts are on shelves and the lower we stoop, the more we get.'
~F.B Meyer

When you enter a supermarket the shelves are all arranged to catch your eye, with a lot of important products just at eye level. It is no surprise that you will find milk, butter and other essentials at the other end of the supermarket, ensuring that you will be tempted to buy as you walk along the aisles. We sometimes look up when we're trying to find God but God is especially close to us in the ordinary and down to earth events of our daily lives. So we don't have to reach for the stars or think that God is distant or removed. We can be surprised at what we'll find in those lower down shelves. God never fails to surprise.

 NOTES:

A Year in Reflection

A windmill farm near Millstreet, Co.Cork

JANUARY 18TH

'Life becomes precious and more special to us when we look for the little every day miracles and get excited about the privileges of simply being human.'
~Tim Hansel

It is easy to take for granted what we have each day. We may not always see today as God's gift to us, but every day is special because of our presence in the world. Our input may seem insignificant but it is significant enough for God to call us special. We are sometimes slow in seeing ourselves as special. We look to others worthy of the title but don't want to apply it to ourselves. 'Special' describes people who act from the heart and keep in mind the hearts of others. 'Special' applies to something that is admired and precious in someone. When we reflect on it a little closer there are no real arguments as to why the title cannot apply to us too. You are special and we thank God for that today.

 NOTES

Rush hour traffic through floodwaters on the Western Road, Cork

JANUARY 19TH

'God does not want us to be in disorder but in harmony and peace'
~1 Corinthians 14:33

If we add some dirt and sand to a glass of water it becomes murky, dirty and looks awful. Give it a good shake and it gets even worse. If we leave the glass for a few hours, the water finds its own balance, the sand and silt fall to the bottom and the water becomes clear again. This is where God always wants us to be. God never intentionally shakes the glass to unsettle us. Life is so unpredictable that the water in our glass can often be cloudy and unclear. Every day we pray to God to bring harmony and peace into our lives. If this seems an impossible task for you today, then it is good for you to know that others are gladly doing it on your behalf. Harmony and peace are precious commodities. They're not for sale but flow from God abundantly.

NOTES:

A Year in Reflection

Floodwaters in the Lee Fields, Cork

JANUARY 20TH

'Imagination lit every lamp in this country, built every church, performed every act of kindness and progress, created more and better things for more people. It is the priceless ingredient for a better day.'
~Henry Taylor

Imagination is the eye of our soul. Without it our lives are dull and lack direction. With a bit of imagination so many things are possible. It allows us to be creative and it gives us the chance to express something that's important to us. Every day is full of possibility and with a little bit of imagination we can put our mark on each day. In our gospels Jesus praised people for their imagination. On one occasion a group of friends lowered their friend on a stretcher down through the roof because they couldn't get in the front door. Jesus was moved by their enthusiasm and the man was healed. If they had chosen to stay outside or come back another day, it may never have happened.

 NOTES

Happy Frogs at Scoil Oilibhéir, Ballyvolane, Cork

JANUARY 21ST

'Lots of people want to ride with you in the limo, but what you want is someone who will take the bus with you when the limo breaks down.'
~Oprah Winfrey

Everyone wants to be our friend when we have everything and when everything is going well for us. But a real friend is someone who will stand with us come what may. It is someone who will walk with us in our darkness, loneliness and pain. It is someone who will encourage us when we're down and someone who will not give up on us when it's easier to quit. Our Gospels remind us of the need to be such a person and especially a person of light, hope and encouragement. As we give to others so we will get back. When we give of ourselves in love we will receive double, treble, quadruple and so much more in return.

 NOTES:

A Year in Reflection

Yellow Himalaya bringing January colour to Fota Gardens, near Cobh, Co. Cork

JANUARY 22ND

'Don't ask what the world needs. Ask what makes you come alive and go do it. Because what the world needs is people who have come alive.
~Howard Thurman

There is only so much time in any given day to get what we want done. The essentials and what needs to be done straight away usually get priority. There are many things we'd like to get around to doing when we get a chance. Often the chance never arrives because it keeps getting squeezed back. This is a pity because these are the things that really bring us alive. They give us energy, enjoyment and really give us the freedom to express ourselves by doing something that we know we're good at. To make the time for these essentials can I get rid of anything I do each day that's not necessary? Am I taking on too much each day? Can I concentrate on something that will make me more alive?

 NOTES

Colourful Bridge on the River Seine, in Paris

JANUARY 23RD

'Circumstances may appear to wreck our lives and God's plans,
but God is not helpless among the ruins.'
~Eric Liddell

We have all grumbled and complained about circumstances in our lives. We sometimes feel that we may have got a raw deal. We sometimes wonder why God allowed these things to happen to us. But what appears broken and lost in our lives, is not so with God. In our brokenness God's love is still working and such love is the greatest healer of them all. We need to be sensitive and compassionate with all brokenness. We need to be patient, courageous and strong. As God gently holds our brokenness, we too need to be gentle with ourselves and with others.

NOTES:

Jet stream from a transatlantic flight, over Tooreenbawn, Millstreet, Co.Cork

JANUARY 24TH

'He has sent me to bring the good news to the poor, to proclaim liberty to captives and to the blind new sight, to set the downtrodden free, to proclaim the Lord's year of favour
~John 2:8-9

It is sometimes hard to change assumptions already made by other people. What we do each day is important but it isn't the only factor in deciding who I am. Much more important is who we are inside and what values are special and important to us. Jesus clearly set his agenda which at its very heart avoids assumptions made by other people. Not everyone is willing to give the poor and the downtrodden their priority. Jesus said it was his starting point. As a starting point today can I appreciate my own inner values? Can I appreciate those that God can bring into my life especially those ones that bring life and energy into my life?

NOTES

Communication Tower on Cork's northside

JANUARY 25TH

'Before I formed you in the womb I knew you, before you came to birth I consecrated you. Nothing shall overcome you, for I am with you to deliver you.'
~Jeremiah (1:4. 17-18)

Someone put it well when they said a Christian should not be a question mark for God but an exclamation point! How often we take for granted what has been given to us. We are reminded just how much we are loved and cherished by God. This didn't happen today or yesterday but happened long before we were even born. We were marked out as special, unique and important. We may fret, worry and fear about many things and yet God reminds us that we will be strengthened for any challenge or difficulty that lies ahead. We can hold our heads up high, be proud of who we are, what we believe in and say that yes our lives are a "!".

 NOTES:

A Year in Reflection

Wave power at Crookhaven, West Cork

January 26th

'Being in the right does not depend on having a loud voice.'
~Chinese Proverb

It would be interesting if the level of our voices could be recorded at a sporting event. Our voice levels certainly go up many decibels, thinking that everyone on the pitch can hear us including the ref! All the shouting in the world can sometimes fall on deaf ears. The same goes with key decisions in our lives. We don't always have to prove a point by making sure we are heard loudly. Often a few words spoken quietly can be just as effective. From a faith perspective, it's not about getting everything just right. Our God is far more understanding than we ever are and knows our limitations better than anyone. It's much more about trying to get it right and thankfully most of us are doing a good job at that.

 Notes

Hanging on at an equestrian cross country event at Garrettstown, Co. Cork

JANUARY 27TH

'As in a game of cards, so it is in the game of life, we must play with what is dealt out to us. The glory consists not so much in winning as in playing a poor hand well.'
~Josh Billings

It would be great if we knew what the next card might be or what life might throw next at us. Unfortunately it doesn't quite work like that. We know from experience just how frail and fragile life actually is. It is in this frailness and fragility that we can somehow find the inner strength to keep going. There is an inner belief within us that somehow things will get better. We believe that it is God who makes all this possible, helping us to make the most of our given situation. We may not be a winner today but God assures us that the real winners are those who are willing to keep all options open even when all seems lost.

 NOTES:

Ancient stone formation at Knocknakilla, near Millstreet, Co. Cork

JANUARY 28TH

'I learned that there were two ways I could live my life: following my dreams or doing something else. Dreams aren't a matter of chance, but a matter of choice. When I dream, I believe I am rehearsing my future.'
~David Copperfield

If we leave everything in life to chance and luck we are going to be sorely disappointed. Hoping for the best and hoping things will work out is inbuilt in all of us, but we need to have deeper roots. It's all about making good positive choices each day. It's all about making a determined effort to choose what I can do well and to avoid tasks that are impossible. It's also about putting our trust in God who has dreams and plans for us too. They are never a matter of chance but always built on the strongest of foundations, Gods deep love for each of us.

 NOTES

Colourful January hedgerow along the Cork-Macroom road

JANUARY 29TH

'Everyone who asks receives.'
~Matthew 7:8

We are always under the eye of a loving and kind God and never a harsh, cold or critical God. That is what prompted Jesus to say, "Ask and it will be given to you." Do we truly believe that what we ask for will be given?

The following may help:

Ask God to guide when we are confused. Ask God to provide when we lack. Ask God to heal where there is illness. Ask God to comfort where there is sorrow. Ask God to strengthen for a hard task. Ask God to lead when paths diverge. Ask God to watch over those who are struggling, lonely or depressed. Ask God to strengthen our relationship with another. Ask God to open new doors and pathways in our own lives. Ask God to transform a negative into a positive. Ask God to help you to be really you.

NOTES:

A Year in Reflection

Kitesurfing near Owenahincha, Rosscarbery, Co. Cork

JANUARY 30TH

'Perhaps only a smile, a little visit or simply the fact of building a fire for someone, writing a letter for a blind person, bringing a few coals, finding a pair of shoes, reading for someone, this is only a little bit, yes, a very tiny bit, but it will be our love of God in action,'
~Mother Teresa

Mother Teresa puts it so well by saying that it's not just a little bit but even a very tiny bit that can make the difference. So often, people think that one has to do a lot, to make a difference. There is a feeling out there that God expects a lot from us. Many feel that they cannot meet this expectation and as a result won't even bother to try. If only they knew what God really wants of us. What God expects of us is far less than we imagine. Why not start today? Not just a little but even a very tiny bit can be a great start.

 NOTES

Winter Wonderland on Mushera mountain, near Millstreet, Co. Cork

JANUARY 31ST

'Every day we are given stones. But what do we build? Is it a bridge or is it a wall?'
~Author Unknown

Every day presents us with so many opportunities. We can either use them to create more opportunities or waste them. A bridge connects, a wall blocks. Each day we are invited to connect with somebody or something in our lives. This seems straightforward enough except that it's much easier to play safe and careful by hiding behind a wall. Today God invites us to cross some bridge in our lives. We may not have all the answers but God always helps us connect with each other and with life. As we leave this month of January, we are crossing a new bridge. We can cross over into February with the building material to build better lives. We ask for God's help and direction as we head for a new month.

 NOTES:

FEBRUARY

St.Brigid's Day crosses

FEBRUARY 1ST

'Reflect upon your present blessings of which everyone has many; not on your past misfortunes of which all have some.'
~Charles Dickens

It's always good to reflect. We often though reflect only on our own misfortunes, our mistakes and all the regrets of the past. Sometimes we even crucify ourselves on all that's gone wrong in our lives, blaming ourselves and others for what has happened. We do it so much that it often clouds all the good around us. Today the feast of St. Brigid is a day to reflect on all our present blessings and all the good around us. She had time for everyone, including the poor, but above all she inspired people to greater things. Using rushes she wove them all into a cross, to remind us that all the different strands of our lives are connected. They are connected not by chance but by the gentle presence of God in our lives. We ask her many blessings on us today.

NOTES:

A Year in Reflection

A candle is lit to mark Cadlemas Day at St. Oliver's Church, Ballyvolane, Cork

FEBRUARY 2ND

'There is not enough darkness in the entire world to put out the light of even one small candle.'
~Robert Alden

Today is Candlemas day and in many churches candles are blessed. These candles will then be used throughout the year for many different occasions. Candles are also used in homes to create ambience and atmosphere. They come in all shapes, colours, sizes and scents.

From a faith perspective candles have always represented the light of Christ. We live in a world that is often darkened by evil and darker forces. We believe that the light of Christ is powerful and strong enough to wipe out all forms of darkness. We have to choose the light, we need to share it with others and we need to be proud of our own light. Today we invite God's light into our lives, into our darker corners and wherever such light is most needed at the moment.

 NOTES

Crocuses in full bloom on the South Link Road, Cork

FEBRUARY 3RD

'Through the intercession of Saint Blaise, bishop and martyr, may God
protect you from all ailments of the throat and from all forms of evil. Amen.'
~Blessing given on the feast of St. Blaise (3rd Feb)

Today is the feast of St. Blaise, whose life was very simple and ordinary. Yet he is known worldwide for his care of those who were sick and particularly those with ailments of the throat. He was a physician who was very close to God. The sick came in crowds to consult him and some even brought animals. St. Blaise cured many people of their ailments and always sent them away with his blessing. He cured not just physical ailments of the throat but spiritual ones as well. Some of these included gossiping, lying and coarse language. Many churches will give the blessing today. If we can't make it to a church, then our own quiet prayer to St. Blaise will be just as effective and important.

NOTES:

A seagull makes a landing on Valentia Island, Co. Kerry

FEBRUARY 4TH

There is a story told about a seagull's first flight. Safe in the cliff, high over the sea, he refused to fly. His brothers and sisters had made the jump and were enjoying life. He'd take a little run to the edge of the nest, look down on the sea miles below, flap his wings and retire in fear. The mother teased the young seagull out of the nest with hunger. She kept dangling pieces of fish in front of him until one day he jumped. With a loud scream he fell downwards into space. His mother swooped near him. He heard the swish of her wings. He was in terror but only for a moment. Suddenly his wings spread out. The wind rushed against his breast feathers, under his stomach and against his wings. He wasn't falling now but soaring with delight.

The invitation is for each of us to also trust our God. Can we take that plunge? Can we trust God to give us that vital lift each day?

 NOTES

Rugged coastline at Lamb's Head, Co .Kerry

FEBRUARY 5TH

'Kevin was a first class pupil at school. His teacher asked the class, "What is the colour of apples?" Most of the children answered "red". A few said "green". Kevin raised his hand and said "white". The teacher tried to explain that apples could be red, green, or sometimes golden but never white. Kevin was quite insistent and finally said, "look inside".

So often we look only to the externals. We judge people by looks, by the clothes they wear, by the colour of their skin, by their accent, by the house they live in, the registration of their car and so on. Often we fail to look within and see the beauty and potential of each person. God always looks beyond the externals and sees the beauty, uniqueness and great potential of each person. We may not be as generous in how we judge people but to look within is always the best way to go.

 NOTES:

A Year in Reflection

A litter of King Charles Cavalier puppies at Kilmorna Heights, Ballyvolane, Cork

FEBRUARY 6TH

A woman brought a litter of King Charles Cavalier puppies to the veterinary clinic for vaccinations and deworming. As the look-alike puppies climbed over and under one another in their box, the vet realised it would be difficult to tell the treated ones from the rest. Putting his fingers into a bowl of water, he moistened the head of each puppy as he finished working with them. After the vet sprinkled the last pup with water, the woman leaned forward and whispered to the vet, "I didn't know they had to be baptised as well!" It may be a light hearted story but sometimes people misinterpret what we do or say as well. We think we are doing what's normal and what's expected of us. But others might interpret our actions differently mainly because they don't fully understand our story or situation. Often there is little we can do but just to know that not everyone is on the same road as we think they are.

 NOTES

Early February buds on this red plant at Tooreenbawn, Millstreet, Co. Cork

FEBRUARY 7TH

'God does not ask you to be a monk or a hermit. You must be silent in the way God asks you to be silent.'
~Vincent Pallotti

Sometimes the thought of complete silence, quietness and time on our own is most appealing. The life of a hermit seems attractive but the reality is that few of us would last even a day! We have grown so accustomed to noise in our daily lives that silence is something that's difficult for most. Yet silence is a precious gift that needs to be experienced little and often. A common link in all of the great spiritual writers is to find that space in our lives which we can claim as our own. When we find that space, even if it's only for a few moments, we can be sure that we are indeed very close to God.

 NOTES:

Elegant and graceful in February sunshine at Ivale, Kilcorney, Co.Cork

FEBRUARY 8TH

'A famous violin maker said the best wood for violins comes from the north side of the tree. The reason is that it has been seasoned by the cold north wind.
And that seasoning gives it a special sound.'
~Mark Link

The same can also be said of us as well. Sometimes the trials and tribulations of life can make us better instead of bitter. A good example is Beethoven. He lost his hearing at the age of 28. When he conducted the first performance of his ninth symphony, he couldn't hear the music, except in his mind. Nor could he hear the thunderous applause that followed. God never intentionally sends suffering or pain to anyone. God never promises to shield anyone from what life can throw at us. But God most certainly has promised to give us strength and courage to cope with all our struggles. We may at times feel abandoned by God but it's at that moment that God is closest to us.

 NOTES

Sheep relaxing on the hills near Glengarriff, Co. Cork

FEBRUARY 9TH

'With a friend your needs are answered. A friend is a field which you sow with love and reap with thanksgiving.'
~Kahlil Gibran

We may have many acquaintances, people we know through work, sport, leisure and just out and about. We sometimes call them friends. But real friends can be counted in one hand. They are best described as people who are genuine, caring, loyal and who will stand by you no matter what. Such friends are rare and precious. Who are my real friends? Have I shown my appreciation recently? What's precious always needs nurturing and care, especially real friends. It would be a shame to take them for granted.

NOTES:

A Year in Reflection

Six Nations Rugby is in full swing. Come on Ireland!!

FEBRUARY 10TH

'There's such a thin line between winning and losing.'
~John Tunis

The Six Nations rugby championship always brings great excitement. Our Irish team have always thrived in these games. But like any sport there is always a mixture of ups and downs, joys and frustrations. Sometimes a win is often so near and yet so far. What happens in sport is so often reflected in life. Just when everything is going well, something seems to happen to pull it all away from us. Disappointments, hurt and pain are something we all have to face. We can't bury or ignore them. We do our best to use them as stepping stones in getting back on track again. Losing is a tough place to be, but the real strength lies in our inner belief that losing is not a cul-de-sac but a stepping stone to better things.

 NOTES

A Year in Reflection

Bishop John Buckley celebrates Mass at the grotto in Lourdes, France

FEBRUARY 11TH

'Love is a medicine for the sickness of the world, a prescription often given, too rarely taken.'
~Author Unknown

Today is the feast of our Lady of Lourdes. It is also world day for sick
people. Today we remember all our sick, in hospitals, nursing homes and
at home. Lourdes in the south west of France is a place where love
oozes, thrives and heals. Everyone is touched in some way by such
genuine love and care. The sick are showered with physical and
spiritual love. The difference that such love can make is something that
touches everyone who visits Lourdes. Not everyone will get the chance
to go to Lourdes. But we can all make sure that God's greatest medicine
called love gets shared, used and above all taken. All of us are
instruments of God's healing love. We pray for our sick today and we
also include all those who look after our sick as well.

 NOTES:

An Angus shows off unusual ears at Tooreenbawn, Millstreet

FEBRUARY 12TH

Once there was a wise old man who lived at the top of a mountain. One day three teenagers decided to trick the old man. One of the boys said, "This old man thinks he knows everything. I'll show him. I'm going to hold a bird behind my back and ask the old man if the bird is alive or dead. If he says it's alive, I'll crush the bird. If he says it's dead, I will let the bird free to fly away." With the plan set, the three boys climbed to the top of the mountain. There they saw the wise old man meditating. The boys walked over to the man and one boy asked, "Wise old man what do I have in my hand?" Because the wise man knew everything, he said, "It's a bird, my son." Now the boy winked at his friend and said, "Wise old man, is the bird alive or dead." The wise old man turned and looked at the boy in the eye and said, "The answer is in your hands, my son."

 NOTES

A motocross enthusiast shows how it's done at Vernon Mount, Cork

FEBRUARY 13TH

'One thing life taught me: if you are interested, you never have to look for new interests. They come to you. When you are genuinely interested in one thing, it will always lead to something else'
~Eleanor Roosevelt

It's a well known fact that life is what we make of it. We can choose to moan, groan and give out or we can choose to do our best, give it a go and make the best of any given situation despite obstacles in our way. No matter what our age there are plenty of opportunities to begin something new, renew something that we liked doing back along or just continue something we enjoy doing at the moment. Thankfully the choices are many today. It is also a well known fact that we can benefit spiritually from wide and varied interests. The inner voice or spirit of each person thrives when it's given the freedom to express itself in something

NOTES:

Teresa and Derek Coughlan celebrate Valentine's Day in style

FEBRUARY 14TH

'God does not love us because we are valuable. We are valuable because God loves us.'
~Fulton Sheen

Today, Valentine's Day, is most certainly a day to feel loved and cherished by someone. Sometimes words like "I love you" can make the world of a difference, lift our spirits and help us to feel loved and cherished. It's a day to celebrate love as a precious gift from God, a gift to be nurtured and appreciated not just on Valentine's Day but indeed every single day. Valentine's Day may have its critics and some will say it's a gimmick but love is far from gimmick. Someone put it well when they said to love someone is nothing, to be loved by someone is something but to be loved by the one you love is everything. We also celebrate today God's unique love for us. We are valuable because God loves us and nothing or no person can ever take that from any of us.

 NOTES

Floodwaters at Doonoure, Kilcorney, Co. Cork

FEBRUARY 15TH

'If we play like that every week we'll get some level of consistency.'
~Alex Ferguson

Few can doubt the genius of Alex Ferguson in his contribution to Man Utd. As a team they have consistently played good football, nurtured great talent and led by example on the playing field. It's not done on the odd week here and there but right throughout the year. Valentine's Day may well be finished for another year but from God's point of view, yesterday was only one day in the whole circle of life and love. Love in all its forms needs to be nurtured and cared for every single day. It's all about consistency and sticking with it. When it's taken for granted we become casual and careless. Love can never be put on a shelf until we need it. Like life, love is the energy and heart beat of life. Today and indeed every day I thank God for its presence in my life.

NOTES:

A winding road heading towards Camp, Co. Kerry

FEBRUARY 16TH

Chris Evert, one of the world's finest tennis players, had tremendous powers of concentration. Like most top tennis players, she started early in life and played the game single-mindedly. Once during a game someone had left a chair near the back line. Whenever Chris went way back for a shot, she bumped into the chair. But she never moved it. After the match, someone asked her why she hadn't moved the chair. Chris looked puzzled, "What chair?" she asked.

There are some people who will complain at the smallest of things. Something small is made out to be a huge obstacle and disturbance. Others simply are more forward, see fewer obstacles and keep going when others get stuck. The Christian call is likewise, keep moving forward when it could be easier to blame, complain and give up.

NOTES

A colourful rainbow at Rylane, Co. Cork

FEBRUARY 17TH

'We are the wire, God is the current. Our only power is to let the current pass through us.'
~Carlo Carretto

The image of the wire and current is an appropriate image. We sometimes forget that we are the instrument. Through us God can do so much. All we have to do is let God flow through us and in all we do. Our lives will be enriched and nourished. But unless we fist turn on the switch the current won't flow. Perhaps an appropriate prayer today might be:

Lord, you are the current and lifeline of my life,
I ask you to give me enough power and energy
to get me through this day.

 NOTES:

Isolated coastline near Ballyferriter, Co. Kerry

FEBRUARY 18TH

'Tell someone there are 300 billion stars in the universe and they will believe you. Tell them a bench has wet paint on it and they will have to touch it to be sure.
~**Murphy's Law**

It is sometimes easier to tell our life story to a stranger than to someone close to us. There is a fear that someone close to us will not fully understand, whereas someone on the outside may be in a better position to listen and understand. We can use our journey through this month of February to see God, not as a stranger but as someone who is close and near. No matter what our story God always understands and never judges or condemns. But like wet paint we're always slow to accept this. We need to touch it to be sure whether it's wet or dry. God is indeed close and near to us. Nothing or nobody can take this away from us.

 NOTES

A young foal named 'Foaly' at Ballyellis, Mallow, Co. Cork

FEBRUARY 19TH

'I am only one, but still I am one. I cannot do everything but still I can do something. And
because I cannot do everything, let me not refuse to do the something that I can do.
~Edward Hale

This quote is a little gem and worth remembering. It takes a bit of
courage to say 'I cannot do everything'. The pace of life today is so
frantic and at times chaotic. We are almost pushed to try and do
everything, accomplish deadlines and deliver on so much. We may be
only a drop in the ocean in the cycle of everyday life but yet what an
important drop we are. God never expects us to do everything and
God never asks us to be perfect. But we can do many things well and
these are what bring life and energy to our lives. Is there anything that I
can do well during this day? It may seem insignificant to you but in God's
eyes it means the world.

 NOTES:

Goats and sheep taking time out at Tooreenbawn, Millstreet, Co. Cork

FEBRUARY 20TH

'Very few burdens are heavy if everyone lifts.'
~S Wise

Trying to carry our own burdens on our own is nearly an impossible task. If we share our burdens with others they will become lighter. We can also help someone else with their burdens, by being there for them, listening to them and simply being a friend. We don't have to have the right words, in fact few are often needed. Our presence with someone else can make all the difference. The danger is that we often leave it to someone else and that someone else is also leaving it to you. We especially remember those beautiful words from our gospel: "Come to me all you who labour and are overburdened and I will give you rest."

 NOTES

White cotton buds enjoying the February sun at Tooreenbawn, Millstreet

FEBRUARY 21ST

'Every believer in this world must become a spark of light.'
~Pope John 23rd

One of the key working parts of a car is the spark plug. It may not be visible externally but internally within the engine it creates a continuous supply of sparks to ignite the fuel and bring the engine to life. The little spark may be tiny but without it all engines will grind to a halt. Each of us can be described as a vital spark of life and light. We need each other for support, encouragement and friendship. We need each other to nurture and share God's light and love with all those whom we live, work and relax with. One spark of light is clearly visible. A few sparks together is the beginning of something. A lot of sparks together generate many possibilities. No spark at all is a great insult to God.

 NOTES:

Prayer books laid out to perfection in the military chapel for U.S. Cadets, near New York

FEBRUARY 22ND

The city, town or village which forgets to care for the stranger has forgotten to care for itself.'
~Greek saying

The Christian response has always put hospitality as treating the stranger as a guest. A stranger has always been described as someone who did not belong to one's clan, one's race, one's family or one's religion. Today our times and culture are marked by a deep ambiguity. There is fear and distrust of any stranger. In Ireland 10% of the population are immigrants. This latest figure puts a fresh challenge before us in how we treat all strangers or immigrants. It is easy to ignore and leave them to others. To ignore them is to also ignore and dismiss God.

 NOTES

Dalmation 'Maxi' is all ready for her walk at Tooreenbawn, Millstreet

FEBRUARY 23RD

'Hope is so much. Hope grows. Hope rejoices. Hope struggles. Hope is challenged but it never dies. It stumbles but it never falls. Hope is life and life is hope. It's always there and always on the move. It is imperceptible or outrageously present. But it is always, always there.
~ Shana Mongwanga

Whatever any day may bring us, we need hope to cling to and give us the inspiration we all need. As believers we firmly believe that hope is rooted in God. On our own we are limited in what we can do. With God as a part of our lives the overall life picture can make better sense. We can never fully understand everything but hope ensures that we accept all the ups and downs of life in a more balanced way. Without hope we are lost but with hope today is a better day.

NOTES:

A surfer powers ahead of the tumbling wave on the Californian coastline, U.S.

FEBRUARY 24TH

'Do what you can, with what you have, where you are.'
~Theodore Roosevelt.

Sometimes simple advice is better than books of great insight. There is much written on how to maximise our time, our profits, our priorities and so on. To maximise anything requires discipline and a sharp focus on what needs to be done. God always gives us more than enough to do our best and get things done. But we miss out on a lot when we try to get everything done today. Today will always be the most important day but it's a day when we can only do so much. Tomorrow will present new opportunities and there will be new things to get done. But that's tomorrow, for now we thank God for our best efforts made today.

NOTES

Snow makes little caps for these daffodils.

FEBRUARY 25TH

'Write down in sand all the bad news and write down in granite all your good news.'
~Old Saying

We probably have grown used to hearing bad news before we hear good news. It's not that there isn't enough good news, it's just that bad news seems to have quicker legs and always gets to be heard first. Your good news should always be appreciated. Hopefully as you look back on your day you will be able to write something good down on granite, something that went well for you, something that you were happy about, something that made today stand out. Whatever was not so good can be written down in sand. Just as a tide washes every sand shore clean, God also wants us to let anything bad or mistakes made behind us. God willingly wants to wipe them away but never wants to wipe away what's written in granite.

 NOTES:

A fir tree bursts into life after the Winter months.

FEBRUARY 26TH

'Yesterday is a cancelled cheque. Tomorrow is a promissory note.
Today is the only cash you have, so spend it wisely.'
~Kay Lyons

Each day is a small fragment of a lifetime. We can't return to the past except within our memories. We don't know what the future holds for any of us. The only time we can spend is today and the only time we can touch is right now. It might seem an oversimplification but so many are either stuck in the past or immersed in what the future might bring. It would seem that today is sometimes forgotten! The best starting point is to see today as God's gift to us. We are invited to use all that's been given to us to enrich our lives, physically, emotionally and spiritually. If we can give all three of these an honest go, then we are indeed living life to its fullest. We are also doing what God wants each of us to do

 NOTES

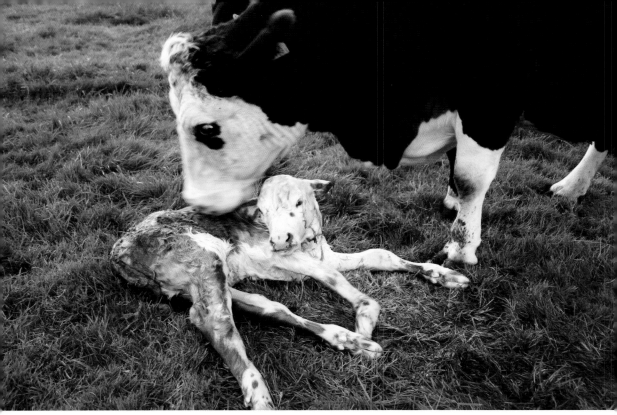

A young calf is only a few minutes old.

FEBRUARY 27TH

'Anyone who keeps the ability to see love never grows old'
~Franz Kafka

As the line from the song goes 'Love is all around'. The problem with our world today is that negativity and bad news stifle all good news including love. Moments of love are what make up each day. It's the little moments that often count the most. We can grow so accustomed to bad news that we can miss many little moments of love. Saying "Thank You", "Well done", "You look great", "Can I help?" are great starters.

A moment in prayer for someone, a sympathy or get well card, a phone call to a friend, a visit to someone in need are other such moments. Love flows abundantly all around. When we fail to see the many little streams and tributaries of love we are very much in a cul-de-sac. As scripture reminds us, where love is, God is also present.

NOTES:

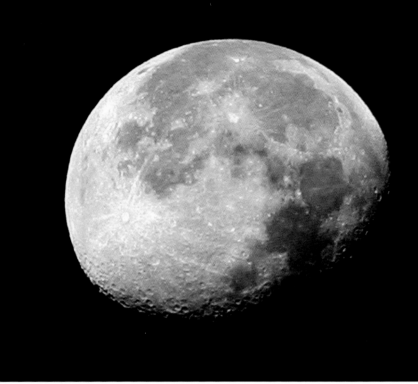

A close up of the moon from Myross Wood Retreat Centre, Leap, West Cork

FEBRUARY 28TH

'I like to think that the moon is there even if I am not looking at it.'
~Albert Einstein

For thousands of years God has been compared to the sun and moon. Just as these are constant so is the presence of God in our lives. On rare occasions an eclipse can occur covering both in shadow. Sometimes too in our lives we can feel that God's light has abandoned and deserted us. But God's light and gentle presence in our lives never leaves us. Just as the sun and moon generate light, day and night, so too God generates so many blessings in our lives. Thankfully these are not as rare as an eclipse but are present in our lives each and every day.

 NOTES

Beauty is in the eye of the beholder!! (Flip book upside down)

FEBRUARY 29TH

'Until you make peace with who you are, you'll never be content with what you have.'
~Doris Mortman

Much of the unhappiness in our world today has its roots in how we see ourselves. Too often we put ourselves down and fall into the tempting trap of comparing ourselves to others. God never makes comparisons or compares us to someone else. We can never live up to being someone else but we can live up to who God created us to be. We can begin this by believing in what we have to offer. It doesn't have to be earth shattering but our little is all that God wants. Others may demand much but never God. God always wants to extend peace to us. Can we make peace with ourselves first? Can we let the negative and cloudy parts of our past behind and move on. It is the only way forward.

 NOTES:

A Year in Reflection

MARCH

Horse riding at Fountainstown, Co. Cork

MARCH 1ST

'To look is one thing. To see what you look at is another. To understand what you see is a third. To learn from what you understand is still something else. But to act on what you learn is all that really matters.'

~Author Unknown

To act on something always requires effort and a determination to make the most of the given situation. But we have often put it on the long finger. We decide that tomorrow will be plenty time or that someone else might do it. If nature decided that tomorrow is plenty of time, we'd have no spring and we'd still be stuck very much in winter. God never asks us to do the impossible. Others may ask the impossible of us, but never God. During this month of March, I can try and accomplish all that is within my reach.

NOTES:

Sweeping countryside at Allihies, West Cork

MARCH 2ND

'We must learn to let go, to give up, to make room for the things we have prayed for and desired.'
~Charles Fillmore

We have all watched a balloon drift up and away. There is something nice about letting it go and watching where it might go. There are also things in life that we need to let go of as well. Letting go doesn't mean giving up, but rather accepting that there are things that cannot be. Letting go of burdens, mistakes made and hurts means that we are willing to move on with our lives. This is far from giving up, but a sign of great courage and bravery. Is there anything in my life that needs letting go? We ask God to replace what we are letting go of with life, light and the possibility of growth/new beginnings.

 NOTES

Snowwhite is all smiles at the Dorset Steam Fair, England

MARCH 3RD

'Jesus took with him Peter, John and James and went up the mountain to pray. As he prayed, the aspect of his face changed and his clothing became brilliant as lightning.'
~Luke's gospel

This piece from Luke's gospel is often called 'the transfiguration'. Right throughout the Gospel stories Jesus himself transfigured people, the broken, the wounded and those lost by the wayside. He touched in on the deepest parts of people and transfigured them by the power of God's love. How can this story apply to us? If we understand the story as all about some form of change, then we are presented with opportunities each day for us to be changed and touched by the power of God's love. God's love can penetrate the deepest of darkness. No story is hopeless or lost, especially ours. The invitation today is to be open to the power of God's love in our lives.

NOTES:

Spring floods at Ballincollig, Cork

MARCH 4TH

'Spring shows what God can do with a drab and dirty world.
~Virgil Kraft

Lent translates as 'springtime'. Everyone welcomes spring; warmer days, the arrival of flowers and new life bursting forth in nature. Lent can also be a time for spiritual growth and renewal. It is always great to be able to open windows on a fine fresh day. You can feel the breeze rushing in to sweep out the stale air. Lent is all about removing what is stale in our lives and allowing life and growth to replace it. Lent is a journey, not just a day or two put together in isolation. As we journey through Lent we invite God into our lives. We especially ask God to replace what's stale and stagnant, with life, energy and freshness.

 NOTES

Pots of daffodils at Altamount, Millstreet, Co. Cork

MARCH 5TH

'The strength you've insisted on assigning to others is actually within yourself.'
~Lisa Alther

We often admire people for what they have achieved and the goals they have reached. We admire their great energy and strength in accomplishing so much. We wish that we could be like them. But while we wish and hope, we forget about our own inner strengths. These strengths are unique to us and make us different from anybody else. If we look around us we can see much of our inner strength in action. It might be at work, at home, at school, at college, some interest or hobby and its something we enjoy doing. It mightn't work for others and what we do may not interest everyone. But most important it works for us and gives our lives meaning and fulfilment. The invitation is to spend less time envying the strength's of others, and nourish the ones that God has given to us.

NOTES:

Fantail Doves keeping a close eye on proceedings at Tooreenbawn, Millstreet

MARCH 6TH

The best way to get to know God is to love many things. Love a friend, husband or wife. Love each day given to you. Love something and you will be on the right way to knowing God.
~Van Gogh

We always need to be reminded how important love is and our ability to love. We can't give it unless we first receive it. Like a radiator it cannot give out heat unless it first receives it. We too must always draw on our supply of love. Love can run dry, but we believe that God always renews and refreshes this supply. Lent has traditionally been a good time for us to renew and refresh. It is easy to grow stale with all things in life, including our spiritual journey. But thankfully it is also possible to get back on track again. It might not happen today or tomorrow, but at least if we're open to something happening, then the chances are good that something will indeed happen.

 NOTES

A Year in Reflection

Richard McCarthy on his horse at Spring Lane, Ballyvolane, Cork

MARCH 7TH

'You cannot pull people uphill who do not want to go, you can only point up.'
~Amy Carmichael

Not everyone agrees with our viewpoints or our approach to certain things. We would like everyone to go with our own ideas, but people do have different and varied viewpoints that need to be respected. We can only put forward our own viewpoint or ideas. We can't force them on anyone. In our Gospels, Jesus never forced his message on anyone and always respected different viewpoints. Unfortunately a close look at Church history will point to the exact opposite. The emphasis was often on fear and punishment. Thankfully the emphasis today is on inclusiveness and respect. It can only begin with ourselves. We can be proud of what we believe in, we can share it with others, we may be enthusiastic or lukewarm about it, but we can never force it on anyone.

NOTES:

West Cork coastline near Castletownbere, Co. Cork

MARCH 8TH

'People are lonely because they build walls instead of bridges.'
~Joseph Newton

We are all familiar with the walls of our own home which are built with great strength to protect and give shelter. However walls can also divide and keep people out. The most famous of them all was the Berlin wall which divided East and West Germany. Thankfully this wall was pulled down back in 1989. It is true that many people are lonely because we spend our time building walls instead of bridges. It is easy to hide behind a wall. But when we exclude other people we are moving away from what God wants us to do. Bridges always connect, unite and bring together. Acts of love, kindness and forgiveness are the best bridges any of us can cross during these weeks of Lent.

 NOTES

'Go on - no one's looking!!' on rocks at Kenmare, Co. Kerry

MARCH 9TH

'You can catch more flies with a spoonful of honey than with a barrel full of vinegar.'
~St.Francis of Sales

It doesn't cost much to be nice, or to make the effort to show our appreciation of someone else. It takes a lot of energy when we are wound up in bitterness, and over time this can take its toll on us. Like a barrel full of vinegar, holding onto bitterness doesn't count for much. Every day God invites us to let go of bitterness, anger and anything that is holding us back. Can we push the barrel full of vinegar to one side and even start with a spoonful of honey? A small gesture of love and kindness today may seem like a drop in the ocean. But in God's eyes, such a drop makes today so worthwhile.

 NOTES:

Stuck in the mud and going nowhere at Tullow, Co. Carlow

MARCH 10TH

'During a storm the cart carrying St.Teresa and her nuns keeled over, depositing them in the mud. 'Pray for us, Mother', begged her nuns. St.Teresa then knelt in the mud and prayed as follows: 'Lord, since this is the way you treat your friends, it is no wonder you have so few of them!' We can sometimes feel that God has seriously let us down. It can happen when a family member or close friend dies. It can happen during an illness or unexpected crisis. We ask the honest question; "Lord, what have I done to deserve this?" There are no easy answers, but God never intentionally sends suffering or pain to anyone. That would be a cruel and harsh God. But we believe that God gives us the strength to cope with all our struggles, pains, hurts, knocks and disappointments in life. When we feel let down, it is then that God is especially close to us.

 NOTES

A Year in Reflection

Jumping clear at hunter trials near Kinsale, Co. Cork

MARCH 11TH

'Every great mistake has a halfway moment, a split second when it can be recalled and perhaps remedied.'
~Pearl Buck

We make mistakes because we are human and because we have our limitations. A mistake happens when we are out of touch with the rhythms of the moment. Or, using an image from photography, a mistake happens when we are out of focus. The halfway moment in any mistake is to look back and say; "What can I learn from that?" Then it's time to move on. There is nothing to be gained from wallowing in self pity and remorse. The Christian response is to use every mistake as an opportunity to be a better and a stronger person. Mistakes can keep all our lives very much in focus and their role may be of greater significance than we had ever imagined.

NOTES:

Bravery:The driver of this car has no fear of making a mistake on the pier at Cobh, Co.Cork

MARCH 12TH

'It is good to have an end to journey towards, but it is the journey that matters, in the end.'
~Ursula LeGuin

Our Lenten journey is an important one. No one is asking us to solve the problems of the world, or do a complete conversion in our lives. If we can use these days of Lent as opportunities to reflect on our own lives, then it is definitely a worthwhile journey. If we can make some improvement in our lives, if we can create some quiet space each day, if we can feel our own goodness and appreciate God's gentle presence in our lives, it will have been well worth it all.

 NOTES

Sam the sheepdog relaxing at Tooreenbawn, Millstreet, Co. Cork

MARCH 13TH

'The purest and most thoughtful minds are those which love colour the most.'
~John Ruskin

We are all affected by colours that we see around us each day. The colour of our clothes often picks up our mood and how we are feeling. Nature provides many contrasts of colours. Different flowers planted in different ways can give many variations of colour. During these weeks of March, clumps of yellow daffodils can really lift our spirits. The same goes for us in relation to colours. On our own we're just one colour, but working together as God's family can bring the best of colours together. We're good at seeing the colours and positives of others, but much slower in believing what we have. The message of the gospels is quite clear. Be proud of who you are, be proud of your colours, and share as many of them as you can with others.

 NOTES:

'We love you' - Yvonne Calnan is very popular with these goats

MARCH 14TH

'To fall is neither dangerous nor disgraceful, but to remain prostrate is both.'
~Konrad Adenauer

Everyone falls and stumbles in life. We all have made some mistakes, done something wrong, messed up big time or regret something we have done. If you aren't in any of these categories then apply to Rome to become a Saint! Much more important for us, is to have the strength and courage to get up and get going again. We can't turn the clock back or undo the past. But today can be a starting point in getting our lives back on track again. We ask God to give us the strength and courage to get up when we fall. Perhaps there is someone we know who could do with a helping hand. A few words of encouragement from us could make the world of a difference.

NOTES

Blackbird at Fota Gardens, near Cobh, Co. Cork

MARCH 15TH

'It takes five years for the seed of a bamboo tree to show any growth above ground, and then it grows to a height of 90 feet in six weeks. Five years of preparation, of putting down roots, of spreading underground, so as to have access to plenty of food. And then, only then, does it take off. So often we expect instant results, today, this minute, right now. But what is special and precious always needs nurturing, care and time. Great patience is often needed. It applies often to people around us. We expect more from them, we want more from them and it sometimes doesn't come. God reminds us to be always patient. Once we nurture and encourage any gift or talent, it will always pay dividends. High expectations and instant results rarely work, but a combination of nurturing, encouragement and patience always go a long way.

NOTES:

Unique parking of a bike on Oliver Plunkett Street, Cork

MARCH 16TH

'When love and skill work together, expect a masterpiece.'
~John Ruskin

We all like doing certain things in life, particularly with interests and hobbies. When we like what we are doing and put our heart into it, the results are often remarkable. This is not just confined to the younger age group. No matter what age we are, if there is a willingness to work at something we enjoy, it should always be encouraged. It's not about perfection or winning all the time. It's all about recognising that such moments are given by God to us. Many of these moments can slip us by because we are so preoccupied with the trivial and unnecessary.

🖋 NOTES

Shamrock is blessed in St.Oliver's Church, Ballyvolane, Cork

MARCH 17TH

'Christ be with me, Christ within me, Christ behind me, Christ before me, Christ beside me, Christ to win me, Christ to comfort and restore me. Christ beneath me, Christ above me, Christ in quiet and in danger, Christ in hearts of all that love me'
~Prayer of St. Patrick

This prayer is one that we could hold close to us, not just today, St.Patrick's Day, but indeed everyday. It's a prayer that reminds us how God is present in the very heartbeat of life. God is close and near to us, not just occasionally, but every moment of every single day. St.Patrick proudly shared this good news with so many Irish people. Sometimes we take for granted our faith and we take for granted so much good news around us. St. Patrick's Day is an occasion to be proud of who we are and what we believe in. Like St.Patrick, we need to concentrate more on the good news around us and much less on all the negative stuff.

 NOTES:

A Year in Reflection

This dog keeps a close eye on the St.Patrick's Day parade in Millsteet, Co. Cork

MARCH 18TH

Reduce, reuse and recycle are words we are hearing a lot more of in recent years. It is all about conserving energy, being kind to the environment and everyone doing their little bit.

Those words can also apply to our spiritual lives as well. The first word, 're-duce', can be used in reducing all those unnecessary burdens in our lives. We are invited to let go and to be open to God's forgiveness and healing in our lives. The second word is 'reuse'. We can reuse what we know to be good, such as kind and encouraging words, healing, letting go, willing to start anew and willing to give someone else a chance. The third word is 'recycle'. Instead of carrying around hatred, bitterness, anger, pain, hurt, resentment, the invitation is to let God do some recycling for us. The invitation here is to be open to God's love, healing and gentle presence in our lives.

 NOTES

A bee returns with pollen to a beehive.

MARCH 19TH

'Blessed is the influence of one true, loving human soul on another'
~ George Eliot

There can be many different types of influences ranging from weak to strong, and from negative to positive/good. The world we live in today is caught up in a lot of negativity. This of course rubs off on us too, but it's up to us to make sure that as little as possible of it gets clung to us. Perhaps we take for granted the influence we have on each other, particularly the good and positive. No matter how ordinary today may be, you will have a unique influence on someone, perhaps without even knowing it. We ask God today to help us believe in our own self worth and our own abilities. May we never take for granted our good and positive influences on other people.

NOTES:

A Year in Reflection

Colourful Waterville, Co. Kerry

MARCH 20TH

'Rest is not a matter of doing absolutely nothing. Rest is repair.'
~Daniel Josselyn

We sometimes underestimate rest in our daily lives. Rest is taking it easy for a while, giving ourselves and our bodies a chance to unwind and relax. It is during this time that our bodies repair, refresh and rejuvenate. Resting doesn't necessarily mean doing nothing. Rest is slowing our pace, becoming less active and less tense. If we look back on any given day we will often see how we are racing around getting things done. It's as if there's some big handout or bonus points if I get everything and as much as possible done today. But it's happening everyday and there seems less time to relax and unwind. Rest is God's gift to you and to all of us. It's a gift that helps us appreciate more of what's around us, and helps us appreciate the gift of this present moment.

NOTES

Daniel & Aoife McSweeney enjoy a lighter moment together

MARCH 21ST

'We can be sure that the greatest hope of maintaining equilibrium
in the face of any situation rests within ourselves.
~Francis Braceland

Today is the spring equinox, with equal amounts of daylight and darkness. From here on we can look forward to much longer days and the arrival of summer. But today also has a spiritual significance. Just like the spring equinox with equal amounts of light and darkness, we are always looking for that balance point. Our lives are hectic and busy and we are pulled in all directions. It is often quite difficult to find some balance and peace. Right throughout our Gospels, Jesus was constantly trying to bring peace, balance and harmony into the lives of many people. It changed their lives for the better. Extremes are never healthy and always best avoided. So we ask God today to help us find the balance point in all we do and in all we hope

NOTES:

Nighttime at Timoleague, West Cork

MARCH 22ND

*'Never give in, never give in, never, never, never - in nothing
great or small, large or petty - just never give in.'*
~Winston Churchill

It's easy at times to get discouraged. It often happens when we compare ourselves to others. It seems they have everything in terms of achievement and success. Just when we're about to throw the towel in, should be the moment when we never give in. Not to give in requires great courage and determination. We ask God to give us the strength and courage to never give in, especially in the face of opposition, a bully, an injustice, peer pressure or some wrong that has been inflicted on us. To do this requires great inner strength and conviction. Asking God to help us means we are half way there.

 NOTES

A deer watches in amusement on Gus Murray's farm, Dunmanway, Co. Cork

MARCH 23RD

*'You can sing about things and talk about things, but if your
actions don't speak louder than words, you're nothing.'*
~Stevie Wonder

We're all good at talking. We may not admit it, but we simply talk and converse about so many things. Some people are bright and bubbly when they speak, others much more quiet and reserved. In God's eyes both styles are important and always bring balance. But at the end of the day, if our actions don't speak louder than our words, then it's all a wasted effort. We so often take for granted the positive influence our life can have on someone else. We may do something very insignificant today but in someone else's eye it can mean the world.

I can talk about anything and everything but unless my life and actions involve love, warmth, understanding and compassion then it's all false and a wasted effort.

NOTES:

Catkins mark the arrival of spring at Aubane, Millstreet, Co. Cork

MARCH 24TH

'If there is one of you who has not sinned, let them be the first to throw the stone at her'
John 8:5

One of the famous and moving stories in our gospels is that of Jesus and the woman who had been caught committing adultery. It is interesting to note that the story is missing from the earliest manuscripts of John's gospel. The delay in accepting the story as part of the gospel reflects the difficulty many people had in the ease with which Jesus lets the woman off the hook. This easiness was totally at odds with the strict penitential practices of the early and later church. Perhaps the church has been slow to accept the heart of the gospel story, slow to accept the readiness of Jesus to forgive. Can we forgive as readily as Jesus forgives? The track record of Jesus on forgiveness is absolutely clear with no strings attached to it. What about our track record?

NOTES

Cows taking shelter from a March shower on Valentia island, Co. Kerry

MARCH 25TH

'Religion is not a way of looking at certain things. It is a certain way of looking at everything.'
~Robert Segal

No one has all the answers or no one ever will. The world we live in today is demanding, challenging and sometimes cruel and unforgiving.
We do our best each day to live in this imperfect world. Most days we do just ok but some days we struggle to cope and survive. Our faith and what we believe in, is a great foundation and a great support in all we do. No religion has all the answers or can claim to know everything. But our faith certainly gives us the chance to look at everything as a whole particularly when the views aren't great in our own life. Our faith gives us a better chance of seeing light, hope and direction around us and will always give us the courage to move forward. At times it may not seem much but it is infinitely better than nothing.

NOTES:

Hen and ducklings on Tomas O'Callaghan's farm, White's Cross, Cork

MARCH 26TH

'Whenever I get full of myself, I remember an elderly couple who approached me in Honolulu with a camera. When I struck a pose for them, the man said,
"No, no, we want you to take our picture!"
~Tom Selleck (Hollywood movie star)

I'm sure we can all relate to similar embarrassing moments. We would gladly have wished that the ground would open and swallow us up. But such moments can often bring us back down to earth. We sometimes get carried away with the busyness of our lives. We can get so involved with different things, that the blinkers are up and we fail to notice what's really happening around us. Sometimes a disappointment or a setback can bring us back to reality. We're not invincible, we do have limitations, and small steps forward are the only way to go.

✒ NOTES

Crows roosting on the Tower-Blarney road, Co. Cork

MARCH 27TH

'Make life easier and lower your crossbar'
~Author Unknown

One of the greatest strains in life is trying to live up to the standards we set for ourselves and those set by others. It is true that a certain level of standards keep us all motivated. But often what we expect of ourselves is simply too high and too demanding. We're not superhuman or never will be. Can we lower our crossbar even one little notch and notice the difference? God also never sets expectations too high of anyone. We are never forced or pushed into doing what God asks of us. It is always open invitation and up to us to do what we can as best we can. Lowering the crossbar is not being defeatist. It is simply accepting that we can often achieve more when we make what happens around us more manageable.

**NOTES:**

A Year in Reflection

Fishermen returning home with their catch to Valentia island, Co. Kerry

MARCH 28TH

The late Cardinal Seunens of Belgium had a friend who spent years looking for a perfect Church to join. He travelled the world and lived with many different communities. Finally he returned to Belgium, admitting failure. His friend the Cardinal said to him cheekily: "I'm not at all surprised, you know. And even if you did find the perfect Church, once you joined it, it would no longer be perfect."

There is a lot of wisdom in that advice. Once we are looking for perfection in someone or something we are going to be sorely disappointed. It is always difficult to live up to high expectations because we all have our weaker points. A great starting point is to acknowledge all our weak points. Then using all our strong and positive attributes, we can use these to build around our weaker points. Such a balanced approach always has the finger of God marked on it.

 NOTES

'Droopy' an Anglo-Nubian goat bonding with her little kid goat

MARCH 29TH

'Love the heart that hurts you, but never hurt the heart that loves you.'
~Vipin Sharma

There are few who go into marriage with divorce in mind. Human nature being what it is, things can, and do, go wrong. Sadly today we hear of many separations, divorces, and often with children stuck in the middle. There is a lot of heartache and pain. The Christian response has always been compassion and to believe in the capacity of people to grow in love. The gift of love needs to be nurtured and treasured every day. Even when all seems lost, even in the middle of heartache and pain, God's love is still present, healing, strengthening, supporting and encouraging. Today we pray for all couples. We pray for anyone going through difficult times, and we include those who have separated or divorced. We pray for God's healing, strength, support and encouragement.

NOTES:

Holy Spirit stained glass window in the North Cathedral, Cork

MARCH 30TH

Many young people have been confirmed during the past few weeks and will continue next month as well. The following reflection are the words of the Holy Spirit to all of us:

When you're lonely, I wish you love. When you're down, I wish you joy. When you're searching, I wish you direction. When you're happy, I wish you contentment. When things get complicated, I wish you simple beauty. When you're angry, I wish you an inner calm. When things look empty, I wish you hope. When you're confused, I wish you understanding. When you're relaxed, I wish you an inner silence.

But most importantly of all I give you my greatest gift, the gift of my presence, that I'm with you right now, during this special day, during the week, during the years ahead. I'm with you always.

 NOTES

A Year in Reflection

A starling picking up straw for a nest at Kilmorna Heights, Ballyvolane, Cork

MARCH 31ST

'It is never too late to be what you might have been'
~George Eliot

One constant theme throughout the scriptures is how God never closes the door on anyone. Even when people tested, ignored and abandoned God, the door was never closed. The very same happens today. God gently reminds us, that it is never too late to be what we were created for. All of us no doubt have things we want to do and we have hopes for the future. Just because things haven't worked out for us back along should not be a reason to throw the towel in. It is never too late to make a fresh start, to retry and to be open to new beginnings. Others may close the door on us, but at least with God the door is always open. Have I thrown the towel in? Do I feel it's too late to restart? Can I begin to trust myself and begin to do something I have been putting off for a long time?

NOTES:

APRIL

Entrance to the tunnel on the Glengarriff/Kenmare Road, Co.Cork

APRIL 1ST

'Stop worrying about the potholes in the road and celebrate the journey.'
~Barbara Hoffman

When we drive into a pothole, we tend to keep our eyes fixed on the road waiting for the next one. When we get a knock in life we tend to expect another one just around the corner. In doing this we forget to celebrate the colour, blessings and joys of our own life. There is much to celebrate around us and much to celebrate today. But if our focus is only on the negative then the smallest of celebrations just can't begin. The following little prayer is appropriate as we begin a new month. Lord, help me to celebrate all the good and positive in my life especially throughout the coming month. It's easy to forget or ignore it, but not today.

NOTES:

Pink flowers by the River Gave, Lourdes, France

APRIL 2ND

'We were born to manifest the Glory of God that is within us. It's not just in some of us, it's in everyone. And as we let our own light shine, we unconsciously give other people permission to do the same. As we are liberated from our own fear our presence automatically liberates others.'
~Nelson Mandela

These beautiful lines are worth reflecting on. Its starting point begins with the vast potential within each person. It's all about confidence.

Am I confident enough to believe that God is a gentle yet significant presence in my life? Am I confident enough to believe in my own light? Am I confident enough to believe in my own goodness? Am I confident enough to allow God to transform my life? The possibilities are endless but I must first be open to them happening in my life.

NOTES

A Year in Reflection

New leaves pushing through at Tooreenbawn, Millstreet, Co. Cork

APRIL 3RD

There's a story told about Mahatma Gandhi who had a visit from a woman who was at her wits end because of the bad behaviour of her young son. The final straw came when he started to smoke before his tenth birthday. "Please, Gandhi, tell him to stop his bad behaviour, be respectful to his mother and give up smoking." "Tell him to come back in two weeks and we'll see," said Gandhi. Disappointed the mother left with her son. Two weeks later they returned and Gandhi put his hand on the boy's head and gently said: "I want you to stop your bad behaviour, to be a good son to your mother and to stop smoking." "I will" said the boy, his eyes lighting up at being spoken to by his hero. The woman was delighted but couldn't resist taking Gandhi aside to ask, "Why did you not do that on our visit two weeks ago. Why did we have to wait?" "Because, two weeks ago, I myself was a smoker."

Are we over generous with advice and suggestions but do not practice what we preach?

NOTES:

Tulips on the Crossbarry/Bandon Road, Co. Cork

APRIL 4TH

'The most valuable of all talents is that of never using two words when one will do.'
~Thomas Jefferson

Gardening centres always do a brisk trade during these early days of April. In every centre there will be a wide selection of plants and flowers. Some will prefer direct sunlight and more will prefer the shade. Those plants that like shade seem to work on a limited amount of light but yet have a vital role to play in any garden or ecosystem. The same goes with prayer. It isn't all about lots of words and long litanies.

Often a few words or even a moment of silence can be the best prayer of them all. During this month of April our focus is not so much on lots of words but on the meaning behind them, Gods love for each of us. No long fancy words can ever take that away from us.

 NOTES

Rainclouds pushing in over Garnish island, West Cork

APRIL 5TH

*'Making the simple complicated is commonplace, making the
complicated simple is creativity'*
~Charles Mingus

We could be called experts in making what's simple complicated and
difficult. So often what should be straight forward in life suddenly
becomes complicated. What started as simple can spiral out of control.
Real individual creativity is making the complicated simple. We need to
push to one side all the unnecessary bits and pieces to reveal the
simplicity underneath. Sounds easy but putting it into practice requires
effort and some divine intervention!

 NOTES:

Boosting germination near Buttevant, Co. Cork

April 6th

'If the source of peace is God, then the secret of peace is trust.'
~ J. Figgis

Everyone longs for peace, peace in our world, our country, our home and especially in our lives. The sense of having peace in our own personal lives is where we have most control and where it is most likely to happen. If it doesn't happen within each of us it won't happen anywhere else. In our Gospels we see how the closest followers of Jesus were not convinced straight away by the Resurrection. In fact we are told they hid behind locked doors such was their fear. Yet they put their trust in God and with time were willing to give their lives for what they believed in. Putting our trust in God doesn't always guarantee what we want. But we are guaranteed a deep sense of peace, belonging and courage to move forward with our lives, not in fear but with great confidence.

 Notes

Views over Bantry Bay, West Cork

APRIL 7TH

'It's really a wonder that I haven't dropped all my ideals because they seem so absurd and impossible to carry out. Yet I still keep them because in spite of everything I still believe people are really good at heart.'
~Anne Frank

Anne Frank's story has inspired millions all over the world. Her personal diary reveals how she was so aware of the powerful force of the darkness of evil during World War II. Yet in the midst of such darkness, pain and worry she truly believed in goodness and love and that everything would work out somehow. We too can sometimes get caught up and overwhelmed by negative news and tragic stories. It's easy to get stuck in a rut, thinking that this is normal, it's not. It never is or never will be. As believers we must always search and nurture good news. The battle between good and evil will always go on. Like Anne Frank we must never give up on good news.

NOTES:

A Year in Reflection

A young lamb relaxes at Mountleader, Millstreet, Co. Cork

APRIL 8TH

'Happiness is neither with us only, or without us. It is the union of ourselves with God.'
~Blaise Pascal

If only we could wave the magic wand and bring more happiness into our world and into our lives. Everyone strives to be happy and much is done to try and achieve this goal. The consumer world with clever advertising creates a shallow message, that if you want happiness then you must buy it. Yet the best of material goods can often mask over an inner loneliness. Real and lasting happiness cannot be bought. Its roots are within each of us and with God. Such a union holds the test of time. It doesn't mean we are shielded from the knocks and bruises of life. But it does mean that we are in a much better position to cope and recover. But most importantly of all such a union puts us in the best possible position for finding real inner happiness.

NOTES

A Year in Reflection

Orange Berberis colour at Tooreenbawn, Millstreet, Co. Cork

APRIL 9TH

What do you have that other people use more than you do?

Answer:

Your name! So often we take our name for granted but it's what gives us our true identity. In Ireland the top five names for newly born boys and girls are: Jack, Sean, Adam, Conor and James: Emma, Sarah, Katie, Amy and Aoife. Sometimes our names are shortened and sometimes nicknames take hold. But every name has some meaning and all have many positives in built. Just as our name marks us out as special, God has gone even further by giving us our own unique fingerprint and DNA. No human hand or machine could ever create such individual marks. Today is a day to treasure your name and why not say a little prayer for those who gave it to you as well.

 NOTES:

A fern pushes forth new growth at Murphy's Rock Valley, Kilcully, Cork

APRIL 10TH

A famous gardener was coming to the village to judge a gardening competition. Most people decided that the result was a foregone conclusion, because the beautiful garden of the manor house had won first prize three years running. For the first time old Joe Murphy decided to enter the competition. His friends laughed at him, saying he didn't have a chance. The night before the judging, there was a terrible gale. People woke to find their gardens battered. The lady of the manor told everyone not to worry, saying she knew the judge personally and he would understand. But Joe got up early, repaired his garden as best he could. The judge came and was so impressed by Joe's willingness to repair such a mess that he was awarded first prize.

We sometimes assume that everything is a foregone conclusion. Like Joe we should never assume anything and simply give each day our best and honest effort.

 NOTES

View from Ceann Sreatha, Dingle Peninsula- Heaven on earth

APRIL 11TH

In the window of a locksmith's shop was a sign: "Keys made while you wait". Business was slow and he tried to figure out what the problem was. He finally decided that people just don't like to wait. So he changed the sign to read: "Keys made while you watch"

Few of us like to wait and of course it's much easier to watch! But notice the difference that one word can make. The power of a single word is something we underestimate. It is a well know fact that we put a lot of emphasis on negative words like can't, mustn't, shouldn't, don't, never. Why not try and reverse some of them? Why not put the emphasis on the positive words, yes I can, I know I can, I will be strong, I will do my best, I will do it... One small change can bring such a difference.

 NOTES:

Jack Frost covers thorny wire at Tooreenbawn, Millstreet

APRIL 12TH

'Self Esteem is so delicate a flower that praise tends to make it bloom, while discouragement often nips it in the bud.'
~Alex Osborn

The arrival of spring is in full swing in the greater Cork area. Beautiful sunshine for the past number of weeks has meant that buds and flowers are pushing forth with great enthusiasm. Frost is the biggest enemy of any gardener during the month of April. It can burn and wipe out delicate buds and seedlings. The same goes for each of us as well. We need to build up our self-esteem and self-worth each day. A few words of praise, encouragement, appreciation and thanks will do wonders in building up our confidence and self-esteem. Words of discouragement, criticism, sarcasm and back-biting are like a bitter spring frost. They wipe out what's precious and delicate. Today I can make an honest effort to praise and encourage those nearest and dearest to me.

NOTES

Sunset over Millstreet, Co. Cork

APRIL 13TH

Simon Peter went aboard and dragged the net to the shore, full of big fish, one hundred and fifty-three of them and in spite of there being so many the net was not broken. Jesus said to them; 'Come and have breakfast'.
~John 21:10-12

There is something so natural about Jesus having breakfast with his closest friends. There was no big fancy restaurant, no fancy knifes or forks, no napkins. Jesus met the disciples as he had always done, in a simple down to earth way. They caught no fish that night, yet at the words of Jesus they caught an abundance. The disciples must have been filled with renewed hope and energy after that encounter with Jesus. We may label it as extraordinary, exceptional and unlikely to ever happen to us. But at the heart of this Gospel story is that God makes the extra ordinary possible in our lives.

 NOTES:

Low clouds near Eyeries, West Cork

APRIL 14TH

'Prayer gives us the words when there are no words. Prayer is not magic. It does not bend the world to our will, if anything it does the opposite. It helps us notice things we otherwise take for granted.'
~Jonathon Sacks

It's sometimes hard to keep up with the pace of life and its expectations. For all of us there is much to be done each day. We end up only getting through some of what we hoped to do in any day. The thought of trying to fit prayer somewhere into our daily routine seems almost a hopeless request. It's not that we don't want to, it just seems impossible to create the space for it. Yet we are reminded that prayer no matter how simple actually enhances our lives. It helps us to notice things that we otherwise take for granted, it helps us to prioritise what's important and gives us renewed spiritual energy that always works to our advantage.

 NOTES

A young duckling taking its first steps at Kilmorna Heights, Ballyvolane, Cork

APRIL 15TH

'Those who speak most of progress measure it by quantity and not by quality'
~George Santayana

Progress in our modern world has been hectic and frantic. The pace of change can be described as wonderful or frightening. There is no denying that we have made great progress in the whole area of technology, quality of living and more opportunities. But have we sacrificed quality for quantity? Have we let go of important values?

Do we prioritise time for each other, time to listen, time to nourish what's important and time to be there for each other. Or are we too busy caught up in the world of quantity instead of quality. God isn't into deadlines, quotas or time constraints. We are encouraged to make quality time and especially to prioritise those quiet down to earth ordinary moments where God is often present.

 NOTES:

Cliff erosion on Ceann Sibeal, Dingle Peninsula, Co. Kerry

APRIL 16TH

'A little boy was sent upstairs by his father to empty the wastebaskets but he returned so quickly that his father said: "You couldn't have emptied all the baskets in this time." "They didn't need emptying Dad," the boy replied. "They just needed stepping in."

There is nothing like a quick response and a quick job. There are many little morals we can take from this story. A big task in our eyes may not be so to someone else. Problems and burdens sometimes just need stepping on. They can seem big and daunting. Yet with a little help they can soon be put in their place. The basket also has a spiritual message. Like a wastebasket there is always room to throw into it the unhelpful things in our lives: greed, selfishness, sin, bitterness, addictions, anger, bullying, dominance and so on. These need stepping on to keep them where they need to be, out of sight and out of view.

 NOTES

Having a closer look at Carrigafooka Castle, near Macroom, Co. Cork

APRIL 17TH

'O that today you would listen to his voice, harden not your hearts.'
~Psalm 95

In Cork we experience mixed weather all year round. Sometimes we get extremes of each but for the most part we do alright. We may give out about rain but without it even the best of ground turns into a desert. Then when the rain comes, the ground is so hard that it can't get through and so it runs away causing flash flooding. The human heart can work in much the same way as well. When we are hard and cold within, we are spiritually stunted, leaving little room for growth. When we are warm, open and genuinely reaching out, then we are indeed spiritually alive and active. If we have any hope of experiencing God's warmth and love, we must experience it ourselves first.

 NOTES:

Tulips at Our Lady Crowned Church, Mayfield, Cork

April 18th

It was very early on the first day of the week and still dark, when Mary of Magdala came to the tomb. She saw that the stone had been moved away from the tomb and came running to Simon Peter: 'They have taken the Lord out of the tomb' she said, 'and we don't know where they have put him.'
~John 20:1-4

It is hard to make sense of a world that has so much darkness, pain, violence and cruelty. How does this all fit into the story of a loving God? Easter is all about how God has shattered darkness and pain. The Easter message is that darkness and evil will never win or dominate. Light, hope and colour dominate at Easter and rightly so. As we journey through these weeks of Easter the invitation is to embrace all the good news around us. Don't make any excuses. Don't delay the celebrations. Thanks to Easter, darkness and evil are reeling.

 Notes

Duck and ducklings near Fossa Castle, Killarney, Co. Kerry

APRIL 19TH

'It's better to make plans for dealing with problems, rather than deal with chronic worry by avoiding them.'
~Doreen Virtue

We're all guilty at some stage of avoiding problems and obstacles. We hope that with time they will simply go away. But we know only too well that they don't and the more we avoid, the bigger the worry burden for us. Another fallacy to kick to touch is that we're the only one with problems. We're not. It is part of human nature that problems arise and the best way of tackling them is to face them head on. Of course this is easier said than done and it requires great courage. Experience has shown that when we hide and avoid we're only storing extra burdens. Right throughout scriptures we find the consoling and encouraging words "Be not afraid, I am with you." Those words take on even more significance as we deal with our own concerns and problems.

NOTES:

Gorse fire at Aubane, Millstreet, Co. Cork

APRIL 20TH

'Everything the power of the world does, is done in a circle.'
~B Elk

From satellite images we know that the earth is round, as is the moon. The wind blows and whirls in circles. Birds build their nests in circles. The sun is circular in shape. All the seasons move in cycles, as do fertility cycles. Water flowing from a sink spins in a circle. Each day can be described in a circle too. We pack so much into each day, some planned, some of it unexpected and some outside our control. If we believe that everything evolves in a circle where does God fit into the whole picture? At the heart of our scriptures is the belief that God's love for us is eternal and constant. Within this circle God treats everyone as equal, with dignity and with respect. God is the centre point of every circle, which means we are always within God's reach, love and care. This is not just occasionally but every moment of every day.

🖋 NOTES

Sunset on the Beara Peninsula, West Cork

APRIL 21ST

'Life is not a brief candle. It is a splendid torch that I want to make burn as brightly as possible before handing it on to future generations.'
~George Bernard Shaw

We often don't realise just how lucky we are. Our lot may seem dull, bleak and even boring. Some think that our problems are a permanent barrier to our ability to enjoy life. While there may be many barriers in life there are only a few permanent ones. The image of light is a favourite in our Gospels and a reminder how we all have the ability to cross barriers. God always wants to nurture, protect and enkindle even the tiniest flicker of light. This is true even more so when that flicker of light is struggling and even seemingly gone. All our lights together can become a splendid torch of which we can be very proud of.

 NOTES:

A honey bee collects pollen from the Horse Chestnut flower

APRIL 22ND

'If Easter is about the cross why all the chocolate eggs?
Because no matter how broken or hard boiled you are, once you taste the true meaning of the
cross, life is a whole lot sweeter'
~Intercom magazine

Easter is not just made up of a long weekend. The Church celebrates Easter for 50 days and it is indeed a special time of year. The Easter message is one that gives us all hope and gives us a timely lift. We all have our difficult moments. We carry burdens, darkness, hurts, pain and disappointments. We're not on our own, every single person carries these. But the Easter message reminds us, that right in the middle of them, there is a promise of new life, new beginnings and a sense of hope and promise. Without Easter we would have absolutely nothing but with Easter we indeed have everything.

NOTES

Heading home through Bantry Bay, West Cork

APRIL 23RD

'The Church has always been a refuge for the weak and not a home for the perfect. From the Lord they will hear no words of condemnation or rejection. They will only hear words of understanding, acceptance and love.'

~Bishop John Buckley

The word Church can mean many different things to people. It is a collection of people journeying together through life, trying to make sense of life from a faith perspective. Some though see this collection of people as being exclusive, hypocritical, out of touch and selective. If this is what makes up Church, then it has no future. Much more important is the sense of belonging and that we're all part of this collection of people that makes up Church. The example that Jesus gave is to include, accept, be open and above all to love. We live in a modern world that is crying out for such a model of Church. A few here and there can't make it happen. We're all a part of our Church.

NOTES:

Easter garden in St. Oliver's Church, Ballyvolane, Cork

APRIL 24TH

Our bodies are 70% water and without it we would die within three days. The earth has plenty of water yet people can use only 1% of it. The rest is either salt water in oceans or frozen in glaciers. Nearly half of the world's major rivers are going dry or else badly polluted. About 33 countries are expected to have water shortages by 2025. Women in Africa and Asia walk on average 6km a day to collect water. 80% of disease in poorer countries is caused by dirty water.
~Trocaire

For many of us we take water for granted. Every time we turn a tap on water flows and in Ireland so much falls as rain! But not everyone is as lucky. The above statistics are certainly food for thought. In our Gospels Jesus said that he was like living water and that like water he brings spiritual life and growth into all of our lives. Equally the call of the Gospel encourages all of us to appreciate God's many gifts and one of those precious gifts is water, so plentiful and yet so scarce.

 NOTES

The Astor liner pulls into Cobh, Co. Cork

APRIL 25TH

'In the day before modern harbours, a ship had to wait for the flood tide before it could make it to port. In Latin this was called: 'ob portu'. It was a ship standing off at port, waiting for the moment when it could ride the turn of the tide to harbour. If the captain and crew missed this moment, then they would have to wait for the next tide to come in. From this came the word 'opportunity'.

Every day God presents us with different opportunities to make today a good day. There are no perfect days, few great days, some awful days and hopefully on the balance of things many good days. Today can be a good day if I can do my best to seize these opportunities that bring the best out in me. To let them slip can allow a good day go to waste. I can do my best to maximise my opportunities today.

 NOTES:

Seals relaxing on rocks near Garnish Island, West Cork

APRIL 26TH

'The greatest weakness of all weaknesses is to fear too much to appear weak.'
~Jacques Bossuet

The strongest link of any chain is the strength of its weakest link. Everyone has some weakness. This can vary from something as simple as a liking to chocolate, to things of a much more serious nature that we call addiction. A weakness whatever its form, need not be a stumbling block or a cul-de-sac. Every weakness can lead us to something better and more positive by trying to overcome the weakness or trying to live with it better. We often judge people and sometimes perhaps condemn people because of their weakness. No one person is invincible, perfect or without their weakness. The message of Easter is to use our weaknesses as stepping stones to something much more positive and better. It's only we who can begin to make that happen.

 NOTES

A piglet having a quiet word with its mum at Muckross Traditional Farm, Killarney, Co.Kerry

APRIL 27TH

'Laughter has no foreign accent.'
~Paul Lowney

The number of languages in our world is enormous, not to mention the number of different accents and variations of the same language. But all over the world laughter speaks the same language and accent. It is always good to hear someone laughing, smiling or chuckling. Our world is very serious and sad. Heavy burdens and extra worries seem to have diluted the opportunity to laugh. Laughter is indeed a gift from God. Spare a thought for a groom at a recent wedding who knelt down with his bride in front of the altar after the exchange of vows and rings. Unknown to the groom, someone had written, "Help" on the sole of his left shoe, and "Me" on his right shoe! It was all taken in good spirit! We can't laugh all the time, but when we can it is good to do so, especially with others.

NOTES:

Cherry blossoms at Knocknakilla, near Millstreet, Co. Cork

APRIL 28TH

'The greatest truths are the simplest and so are the greatest people.'
~Julius Hare

Big is always impressive and appealing but small can be just as effective and more direct. In the bigger picture our small contribution to life may seem insignificant, yet it is the most important of all. Scripture refers to our contribution as being 'the corner stone' or 'foundation' of life. Do we really believe this? Why does it seem that everyone is doing their level best to make life more complicated? The more complex we make life, the more we struggle to find balance and inner peace. Sweeping changes never work successfully but is there one simple positive change I can make in my life this day? Make it your corner stone today and you will have done a great days work

 NOTES

Heaven on earth, near Castletownbere, West Cork

APRIL 29TH

'Thomas, called the Twin, who was one of the Twelve, was not with them when Jesus came. When the disciples said, 'We have seen the Lord', he answered, 'Unless I see the holes that the nails made in his hands and can put my finger into the holes they made, and unless I can put my hand into his side, I refuse to believe'
~John 20:23-25

We all have our doubts and questions. That's why we should not be so hard on Thomas better known as 'Doubting Thomas'. He holds all our questions and doubts. The message is not to be discouraged. Hold onto them, live them and give them time. This is what Thomas did and marked him out, not just as a believer but marked him out as an open, honest and genuine believer. God always appreciates such openness and honesty.

 NOTES:

A field of oil seed rape at Shanagarry, Co. Cork

APRIL 30TH

'Why is it that it seems to be so much easier to get caught up in the hard things and the
struggles than it is to remember the happy moments?'
~Joyce Rupp

It is sometimes hard to gauge how many people really feel the joys and
blessings of Easter. Illness, tragedy, anxieties, family and personal troubles
can all dampen our enthusiasm for Easter. A better approach as we
leave this month of April and move into May, might be to celebrate the
'little Easters' of our daily lives. We do so by noticing all the insignificant or
little things that happen in any given day. It is so easy to let bigger events
or problems cloud all these simple and precious moments. Some may
see them as insignificant but these 'little Easters' can generate much life
and hope in our own personal lives.

 NOTES

May

Bluetit with caterpillar to feed its young at Kilcully, Co. Cork

MAY 1ST

A Prayer as we begin this month of May

Lord, I give you my hands to do your work.
I give you my feet to go your way.
I give you my eyes to see as you do.
I give you my tongue to speak your words.
I give you my mind that you may think in me.
I give you my spirit that you may pray in me.
Above all I give you my heart that you may love in me.
I give you my whole self that you may grow in me,
so that it is you Lord Jesus,
Who live and work and pray in me. Amen.

 NOTES:

Lots of rocks and stones on a beach in the Dingle Peninsula after some heavy winter storms

MAY 2ND

'Advice is seldom welcome and those who want it the most always like it the least.'
~Philip Stanhope

There is a world of a difference between genuine honest advice and the advice that comes from someone who thinks they know it all. It goes full circle. As children we eagerly acted on the advice of our parents. As teenagers we cringed and ran a mile. As we grew older we began to accept their advice as honest, helpful and at times inspirational. Finding the balance is a daily challenge. We can give advice but we can never force it. We can hear advice from others, reflect on it, accept it or reject it. But before we reject advice it is important to know that every single person has a blind spot. We can never see the whole picture. Advice whether we like it or not is an attempt at showing the whole picture. We ask God to help us in making right decisions and to help us see the full picture at all times.

 NOTES

Maxi (Dalmation) catches up on all the local news!!

MAY 3RD

'The reason why a dog has so many friends is because it wags its tail instead of its tongue!'
~Marie Sheehan

Our gift of speech is indeed wonderful. Words can be used in such a variety of ways, especially to uplift, encourage, console and give thanks. But we don't need a reminder to know how poisonous our tongue can be too. We can all recall times when we have said something and know that as soon as the words left our lips we had regrets. Such words can knock, cut, swipe, hurt and destroy a friendship or relationship. The next time we see a dog wag its tail, will be a reminder of what we should be doing! In our Gospels we never find Jesus gossiping or speaking maliciously about someone. Sure he challenged, but always chose words to uplift, encourage and give hope. Today I can watch how I use my words especially when I use them negatively. Can I make a change?

 NOTES:

Camogie action in a championship game- Newcestown v Bishopstown

MAY 4TH

'Leadership isn't about being the best, it's about bringing out the best in others.'
~Author Unknown

Everyone likes to be the best. In sport being the best brings great rewards. There is an old saying that says, winning isn't everything. The same can be said of being the best. Not everyone can be the best. Much more important is the ability to do our best and the ability to bring the best out in other people. This is at the heart of the Christian message. So many people are full of love, kindness and genuine good will. Just as fruit needs sunshine to ripen, we need some encouragement to bring the best out of us. Being the best is great but bringing the best out of others and ourselves is what it's all about. Can I do something today that will bring the best out of someone in my life?

 NOTES

Colourful roadside on the Watergrasshill by-pass, near Cork

MAY 5TH

A man had the job of painting the white line in the middle of the road. The first day he painted 25 metres. On the next day he painted 15 and on the third day only 8 metres. The foreman came along and asked him to explain why he had slowed down. "Well" said the man, "The can of paint was getting further and further away"!!

Sometimes we also allow God to slip further and further away in our lives. It's not that we intentionally set out with this in mind but quite simply we drift. We move on in our lives, we make new friends, we embrace new opportunities and sometimes we forget to bring God with us. The invitation each day, whatever way its going, is to invite God in.

Using the image of the can of paint, the invitation is to also bring God along with us. We will not be disappointed.

MAY 5TH

 NOTES:

Sheep grazing on the hills near Gougane Barra, West Cork

MAY 6TH

esus said "The sheep that belong to me listen to my voice.
I know them and they follow me."
~John 10:27-28

Today with mobile phones, modern technology and computers we find it more difficult to relate to the image of a shepherd and sheep. Back in the time of Jesus a shepherd was an important member of every community. Sheep were always vulnerable from an attack by wolves. Sheep could easily stray and get lost. A good shepherd watched their flock carefully, knew each one individually, could call out their name and they would respond. Like a sheep we too can stray, get lost and fall by the wayside at times. We too are vulnerable but God is always watching and caring for each of us. When we stumble and fall we are gently lifted up and brought to safety. We may forget God in our lives at times but God never forgets us.

 NOTES

Early silage cutting by John Geaney contractor on Edmund Linehan's farm, Ballinahina, Cork

MAY 7TH

Silver often takes second place to its neighbour gold. It is cooler, shinier and often purer than gold. The vast majority of cups used in sporting competitions are made from silver. One unusual quality of silver is its ability to kill bacteria when it comes into contact with it.

It's as if bad things cannot survive in silver or around it. It should come as no surprise to know that God has often been compared to silver especially in the psalms. Like silver God can be described as "cool". This is the greatest compliment especially in the eyes of a child or young person! Just as silver can kill bacteria, so God can help us control or get rid of negative forces in our lives. Asking God to help us each day, is always positive and a healthy thing to do. To do so means that negative stuff finds it harder to get a foothold. Like silver we have a lot going for us. In fact much more than we think we have.

NOTES:

The Bernard Family surrounded by dazzling oil seed rape at Riverstick, Co. Cork

MAY 8TH

'Love is the flame that warms our soul, energises our spirit and supplies passion to our lives. It is our connection to God and to one another.'
~Elizabeth Kubler-Ross

It has been said that faith makes all things possible but love makes all things easy. Love heals everyone, not just those who receive it but those who give it as well. The word love though is thrown around like a rag doll and we're sometimes part of it. When we say "I love a TV programme" or "I love those shoes" or "I'd love to go for a walk", we are doing an injustice to the real meaning of love. Real and genuine love doesn't just happen. We have to make it happen. Love gathers into a great positive energy when it's connected with God. The invitation each day is to harness God's love in our lives and to nurture every available opportunity to share that love with each other

NOTES

Sailing beside Dursey Island, West Cork

MAY 9TH

'Greatness is not in where we stand, but in what direction we are moving. We must sail sometimes with the wind and sometimes against it. But sail we must and not drift, nor lie at anchor.
~Oliver Holmes

There is nothing worse than drifting along in life. It is easy to let others dictate the pace of our lives and leave them influence our lives. The Christian response has always been to move forward in hope, to be positive about our lives and to trust that God is on our side when the wind is with us, but also when the wind is against us too. Sometimes we find it difficult to initiate a prayer. This little one is a great starter, "Lord, you are the wind in my sails. It is you who gives my life direction. Help me to avoid drifting and help me to move forward in hope."

 NOTES:

MAY 9TH

A Year in Reflection

Mixture of cloud and sunshine at Tooreenbawn, Millstreet, Co. Cork

MAY 10TH

'I have known shadow, I have known sun and now I know these two are one.'
~Rudyard Kipling

Every day is a contrast between light and darkness and between colour and shadows. Nature always finds the balance point especially as the seasons evolve and merge into each other. In our own lives we are not as comfortable in finding the balance. We all find it difficult to find the balance between what goes well and what's struggling for us. There are few whose lives are just sunshine. Every person has some shadow that follows them. We always have to remember that for every shadow, the sun is never too far away. At the heart of our Gospel message is how God journeys with us, even in the middle of our darkest moments. We are reminded that good never looses grip even when our darker moments seem to have a firmer grip.

 NOTES

A fly takes a rest in Fitzgerald's Park, Cork

MAY 11TH

'A little boy was sitting watching his Dad working on the car. The boy noticed that his father had a few grey hairs and he asked "Dad, why are some of your hairs white?" His father answered, "Well son, every time you do something wrong and make me unhappy, one of my hairs turns white." The boy thought for a while and then said, "Well then how come all of Granddad's hairs are white!!!"

There is nothing like a bit of honesty and a bit of humour! We sometimes underestimate the power of speech and the impact of our words. We sometimes use words to gain advantage but it doesn't always work in our favour. When we use words, no one gets it right all the time. What we say can be interpreted by someone else, in completely the opposite way to what we might expect. We thank God for the gift of speech and our unique ability to communicate with each other as best we can.

 NOTES:

Ragwort proving it can grow just about anywhere even on a pillar.

MAY 12TH

'Once you choose hope, anything's possible.'
~Christopher Reeve

A boy was in the burn unit of a hospital for many weeks making very little progress. His teacher was asked to visit him and tutor the boy with some schoolwork while he was in hospital. As she tried to tutor him it was obvious the boy was in a lot of discomfort. The teacher felt ashamed of putting him through such a senseless exercise. The next day the nurse asked her: "What did you do to that boy? His entire attitude has changed. It's as though he has decided to live." A few weeks later the boy explained that he had given up hope until his teacher arrived. "They wouldn't send my teacher to work on nouns and verbs with a dying boy, would they?" We too journey into people's lives and into places and events that on the surface seem to have no meaning or purpose to us. Yet God gently works through us, creating many surprises and in ways we least expect.

NOTES

Laura Murphy all smiles with her horse who thinks its lunchtime!

MAY 13TH

'Being happy doesn't mean that everything is perfect.
It means that you've decided to look beyond the imperfections.'
~Author unknown.

Everyone is searching and looking for happiness. The advertisers of this world tell us that happiness is to be found in the perfect gift, the perfect car, the perfect outfit, the perfect holiday. But there's no such thing as perfect in this world. We live in an imperfect world and there will always be limitations and stumbling blocks in all of our lives. God gives us the freedom to find happiness when we settle for less than perfection. This is not to be confused with settling for something bad but in knowing that 'just perfect' doesn't exist.

NOTES:

A wren watches its home carefully at Tooreenbawn, Millstreet

MAY 14TH

'God gives every bird its food, but does not throw it into the nest.'
~Author Unknown

Many of our gardens during this month of May have birds flying back and forth to nests feeding their young. Countless trips each day are made and nature always provides. God also provides for each of us but we too must play our part. If God did everything we could easily become complacent, self centred and selfish. When I make an effort to do my bit and do my best then we can be assured of God's many blessings. But all the blessings in the world won't make much of a difference unless I am first open to receiving them.

 NOTES

Two cygnets going for a closer look underneath at Oysterhaven, Co. Cork

MAY 15TH

Little Johnny asked his grandmother how old she was. Granny answered "Forty nine and holding". Johnny thought for a moment and said "and how old would you be if you let go?!"

Perhaps we are shy about our age but no matter what our age we are all guilty of holding. We hold on to possessions, clutter, mistakes made, bad memories and much more. Wouldn't it be great if we could let a lot of these go. Why hold onto them? The more we hold on to, the harder it is to move forward in our lives. Today I will think about things in my life that I am holding onto and should let go of.

✐ NOTES:

Carpet of bluebells at Courtmacsherry Woods, West Cork

MAY 16TH

'I give you a new commandment, love one another just as I have loved you.
You must also love one another.
~*John 13:33-34*

Love is indeed a powerful force but we can also miss out on all that love has to offer because we are simply too busy. Love is too precious to ignore especially God's love. It is the greatest thing that God can give us and it is also the greatest thing that we can give God. Perhaps Mother Teresa sums it up best. An American journalist was watching Mother Teresa as she cared for a man with gangrene. He said "I wouldn't do that for a million dollars." She replied, " Even I wouldn't do it for that amount! However I do it out of love for God."

NOTES

A giraffe poses nicely at Fota Wildlife Park, near Cobh, Co. Cork

MAY 17TH

'Prayer is the sum of our relationship with God. We are what we pray. The degree of our faith is the degree of our prayer. Our ability to love is our ability to pray.'
~Carlo Carretto

Thankfully prayer is unlimited. We can pray where we want, when we want and for as long as we want. It seems clear that the pay off from prayer is substantial. There are few experts in prayer. It would be foolish to compare ourselves with their high standards. It would also be foolish to think that we can't do it or that we need some course or degree to get going. The best approach is to make some little time each day for whatever form of prayer works for us. Everyone does it in a different way but all compliment each other. We work through many activities in any given day. Few can match the benefits of our own prayer time.

 NOTES:

Near perfect conditions for a game of golf at Glengarrif, West Cork

MAY 18TH

'God has not called us to see through each other, but to see each other through.'
~Author Unknown

Everyone needs a helping hand. No one should be too proud to think that they do not need help. It may be the start of summer, but for everyone it's not always sunshine. We all have our moments when we need a helping hand. Sometimes we may feel that others don't care or that they won't understand. Sometimes we may even feel that my story is so complicated that it's hardly worth the start. It's important for us to know that a gentle helping hand is out there. It can and will make all the difference, in getting us back on track and going again. The words of Jesus give us all comfort, "Come to me, all you who labour and are overburdened and I will give you rest." We are never on our own. The Samaritans are always available on 1850 60 90 90

NOTES

Breakfast time at Golden Gate Park, San Francisco, US

MAY 19TH

'What we think, what we know or what we believe in, is in the end of little consequence. The only consequence is what we do.'
~John Ruskin

First and foremost in life, we are what we do. If we do our best to be good, honest, generous, loving and so on, then it becomes a part of us. If we decide to be constantly negative, unhelpful, hurtful, sarcastic and so on, then it also becomes a part of us. What we do each day can have such an impact and influence in our world. God calls us to leave our mark in all we do. It is so much easier to do this when we are trying to do our best, when we are trying to live good Christian values and when others believe in what we are doing. If science tells us that every action has an equal and opposite reaction then it is up to us to maximise the opportunities to extend, goodness, generosity and above all love.

 NOTES:

A dandelion seed gently moves on one at a time.

MAY 20TH

'Life is not measured by the number of breaths we take, but by the number of moments that take our breath away.'
~Author Unknown

So often we take our breathing for granted but it is our vital life line. When we are excited, angry or exercising our breathing quickens and when we are relaxed, it, of course, slows down. The image of our breath being taken away by a significant moment is meaningful. Friendships, relationships, words of support and encouragement, kindness and a helping hand can often spark moments that will take our breath away. They rarely are planned carefully but usually happen naturally and spontaneously. Perhaps we don't appreciate them enough for what they are. There is an even bigger chance how we might forget, that in the heart of them is the gentle presence of God.

 NOTES

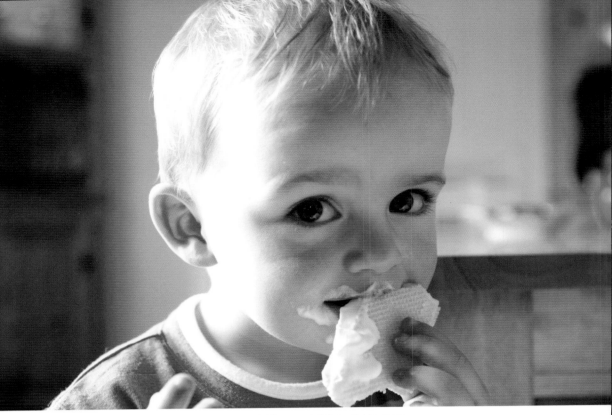

Peter Wills enjoying his ice cream at Altamount, Millstreet, Co. Cork

MAY 21ST

'I was a revolutionary when I was young and all my prayer to God was 'Lord, give me the energy to change the world.' As I approached middle age and realised that half my life was gone without me changing a soul, I changed my prayer to, 'Lord give me the grace to change all those who come in contact with me. Just my family and friends and I shall be satisfied.' But now that I am in my latter years and my days are numbered, my one prayer is, 'Lord give me that grace to change myself.' If I had prayed for this right from the start I should not have wasted my life.

~Bayazid

It would be a shame at any stage to say that we have wasted our lives. We can't change anything in this world or those around us, unless we first are comfortable with change in our own lives.

NOTES:

A starling passes a juicy worm to its young at Tooreenbawn, Millstreet

MAY 22ND

'It is never the wrong time to do the right thing.'
~Author Unknown

As the old saying goes, 'there is a time and a place for everything in life.' This includes a time to do the right thing. Sometimes we're not sure what the right thing to do is and at other times it is very clear and obvious. But even when we know what the right thing to do is, we're sometimes slow and stubborn to do it. This is where prayer can be a great catalyst. Prayer, no matter how simple, can kick us into action.

A simple prayer might be to ask God for the strength and courage to do the right thing or make the right decision. There is never a wrong time to begin such a prayer.

 NOTES

Summer colour kicking in at the bottom of Dublin Hill, Cork

MAY 23RD

'Boredom is the feeling that everything is a waste of time.'
~Thomas Saes

Sport in all its variety brings some great action, excitement and tension. Even from the sidelines it feels as if one is in the thick of the action. The word boring rarely comes into sport. But sadly more and more people today are bored with life, with their jobs, with family life and so on. There is a sense of being limited, of nothing happening and unlikely to happen. Being bored is an insult to ourselves but also to God. Each of us has been created with huge potential and with a reservoir of gifts and talents. There is much to do and see each day. Nothing is ever a waste of time, especially in God's eyes. Every day can be made memorable and special when we maximise all that's available to us each day. Today I can give 'boredom' that sinking feeling.

 NOTES:

MAY 23RD

The Gearagh has its own natural beauty near Macroom, Co. Cork

MAY 24TH

'A new broom sweeps clean, but the old brush knows the corners'
~ *Irish Proverb*

Much money is spent on the purchase of new products. Cars are constantly evolving and changing. Televisions are now sleek and slimline. Mobile phones have got smaller and smaller. The manufactures say that if they stay with exactly the same product their sales will collapse. Something new is always fresh and appealing. But we also can't simply ignore what is old either. No money can buy experience and the wisdom of simply having been there and learnt from all that's gone on before. Spirituality is also built from solid foundations. There is a deep and rich wisdom from all that has been passed on and at the same time there is an invitation to be open to all that's new and refreshing in our lives as well. Nourishing the spiritual side of our lives is the best investment any of us can make.

NOTES

Orange ball and skyline at the top of Dublin Hill, Cork

MAY 25TH

'It is tempting to deny the existence of evil, since denying it gets rid of the need to fight it,'
~Alexis Carrel

In nature birds and animals have over the years adapted to their environment. Many have colours that camouflage themselves from danger. They become one with the colours of their surrounding environment to give them a better chance against predator attacks. It is fair to say that the forces of darkness and evil are always lurking around. Such forces always try and smother goodness, love and light.

As believers we are always in a much better position to counter such forces. We can camouflage ourselves in God's love and protection of us. This does not mean that we are running for cover, merely asking God for protection against forces greater than ourselves.

NOTES:

'Everyone in Cork plays hurling - including me!'

May 26th

'You don't get harmony when everyone sings the same note.'
~Author Unknown

Life would be very dull and boring if we all sung from the same hymn sheet. The old saying 'variety is the spice of life' is a classic. At its heart, it means that we need to respect differences and that others are entitled to different views. Sometimes we expect those closest to us to follow suit and do everything that is special and important to us. Parents will often say "My children aren't going to Mass. What have I done wrong?" The answer is simple: You have done absolutely nothing wrong. You have led the way by example and love. God loves you deeply for what you have done and for what you are doing. Continue doing so because God works in mysterious ways. What you may see as a disappointment, God sees as a glorious opportunity. God isn't into a single note but simply loves harmonies. We're all a part of that harmony.

 Notes

A flower makes its home on a rock at Millstreet Country Park, Co. Cork

MAY 27TH

'An instant of pure love is more precious to God and the soul, than all other good works together. Often it may seem as if nothing were done.
~St. John of the Cross

It is often the case that we underestimate the potential of the little and small. Our day is predominantly made up of what's ordinary and routine. Any little moment where love is the starting point is precious and unique. Put a few of these moments together across any day and you have something special. Sometimes they may seem almost insignificant, common and hardly worth the effort. Yet such moments have the finger of God on them. These moments are the heartbeat of life and the heartbeat of God. They are worth celebrating every single day.

 NOTES:

A colourful Clematis making a statement at Tooreenbawn, Millstreet

MAY 28TH

'Life is like a book that never ends. Chapters close, but not the book itself.'
~Marianne Williamson

There are lots of books in many of our bookstores. Some of these are best sellers and many more hope to follow in the same direction. Every book is different, with a unique storyline and a unique finish. Our lives are like a book and each day makes up the chapters. Some of these chapters are lively and exciting, more are plain and predictable. There are also chapters in our lives that need closure and with closure comes the invitation to start something new. God is always gently inviting us to see each day as a fresh beginning. Today is always the most important chapter. It is a vital link in our life story. Any attempt by us in trying to make today worthwhile makes it a great chapter. There are many great chapters waiting to be written, starting with today.

 NOTES

A butterfly busy on a thistle at Coomathrush, near Millstreet, Co. Cork

MAY 29TH

'It's a small world but I wouldn't want to paint it!'
~Steven Wright

We often talk about how small our world is, especially when it comes to communicating by phone, texting, emails and so on. Air travel has also made access to every country in our world so much easier. But our world is still a vast place. The population is just over 6.5 billion or 6,500 million people, which is staggering. There are 193 countries in the world and 6,800 known languages. There is such a variety of cultures, customs, traditions and religions all over the world. We are also aware of many countries and people struggling, many living in extreme poverty and many dying from hunger. No one person can solve the problems of the world. To try and even think of everything together is overwhelming. All change has to start with ourselves before it can ever take hold of the world we live in.

NOTES:

Aine Cummins and Claire Herbert modelling the Cork hurling team jerseys

MAY 30TH

'The worst moment for an atheist is when he/she feels
grateful and doesn't know who to thank.'
~Wendy Ward

No matter what our age, we are aware that every day has an element of surprise. We don't know what to expect, not just in our lives but especially in the world around us. Each day brings a unique measure of challenges and successes and its own measure of the unknown. No matter how difficult or challenging a day might be there will always be a moment to be grateful for. It mightn't be an earth shattering moment or one that will make the headlines. But nevertheless these precious moments always have a divine origin. We pause each day to thank God for these moments.

 NOTES

Fungi goes for a splash at Dingle, Co. Kerry

MAY 31ST

'The purpose of life is to discover your gift. The meaning of life is giving your gift away'
~David Viscott

How do we know when we have truly discovered our gift? How will I know that this is really my gift? Very few do because each day presents us with a new gift waiting to be discovered. As believers we believe that life is a journey, waiting to be discovered each day. Our gift in life is to believe in ourselves, to believe in our potential, goodness and love, to use all our stumbling blocks we encounter as stepping stones and to believe that God walks with us on this journey. We can't ever hoard or lock away God's blessings in our lives. Our greatest discovery is to know that this supply is endless. Our gift is to appreciate these blessings, live them, love them and even give them away.

MAY 31ST

NOTES:

JUNE

Twin Fuschia on Garnish Island, Cork

JUNE 1ST

A Prayer for the coming month of June

Lord, just as a flower can radiate its precious beauty
and cast its fragrance everywhere.
So I ask you to cast the sweet fragrance of your presence over me.
Surround me with your love.
Fill me with your healing balm.
Enfold me with your peace.
Comfort me with your presence.
May your fragrance linger in the stillness of my soul.
May your healing love renew my very being. Amen

 NOTES:

Sciath na Scoil celebrations at Páirc Uí Rinn

JUNE 2ND

'Don't ask for the task to be easy. Ask for it to be worth it.'
~From the St. Patrick's Missionary Society Calendar

We all have different tasks to do each day. Some are routine, some are necessary, some are burdensome and some are well worth the effort.

There are few tasks that are easy. All require effort and a willingness to give it a go. Difficult tasks are always possible if we take it one step at a time. At the heart of the Christian message is to ask God for the energy, courage and direction in all the tasks we do each day. The greatest satisfaction we can get from any of these tasks is to be able to say it was well worth the effort. Today we ask God's help, not so much in getting the big tasks done, but to be able to do the smaller ones well. Doing the smaller tasks well puts us in a much better position to tackle the bigger ones.

 NOTES

Colourful delicacy at Tooreenbawn, Millstreet, Co. Cork

JUNE 3RD

'If you are lucky enough to find a way of life you love, you have to find the courage to live it.'
~Author Unknown

Today is the anniversary of a young priest Fr. Ragheed Ganni who was gunned down in Iraq along with three deacons. Their killers demanded conversion to Islam and then shot the four repeatedly. Living and working in Iraq meant that Ragheed was living very much in a danger zone. He was asked how he could find the courage to work as a priest in Iraq. He said: "Every time I celebrate Mass, I feel that it is not so much that I am holding the body of Christ but that it is Christ who is holding me." What a beautiful image and one that we could hold on to also. It means that it is Christ who holds us each day and holds us lovingly. He holds our concerns, our worries, our frustrations, our joys and our disappointments. Nothing is ever too heavy for him to hold.

 NOTES:

Windsurfing at Eagle Point, Ballylickey, West Cork

JUNE 4TH

'The first step to improvement, whether mental, moral or religious is to know ourselves, our weakness, errors, deficiencies and sins. It is then that we can begin to turn from them.'
~Tyron Edwards

Sumo wrestling is popular in many parts of the world but in Japan it is their national sport. Each tournament has four awards, (1) winner, (2) outstanding performance award, (3) skill award, (4) a fighting spirit award. It is not just about winning but also about nurturing improvement. It is the main reason behind Japanese prosperity. In terms of spirituality we could also use such a mindset. There is no such thing as a perfect spiritual journey and therefore few winners. But there are many putting in great efforts in doing their best. Small improvements on any spiritual journey are the spice of life. We don't have to go to Japan to nurture those small improvements in our lives.

 NOTES

A fly settles among raindrops

JUNE 5TH

'In one drop of water are found all the secrets of the oceans.'
~Kahlil Gibran

A single drop of water can easily be dismissed. It may not seem much, even beside other drops. Yet it has a valuable role to play and when it joins with other drops, it takes on a new lease of life.

The same also applies to our own situation and particularly those times when we feel we're just a number or lost among so many people. God lovingly knows us by name and knows that within each of us are endless possibilities. When we work together with others, those possibilities become possible. A good start for a prayer might be: 'Lord, help me to realise that I may just be one, but I am an important one. I have a valuable role to play in the world I live in today. Give me hope and confidence to believe in my own ability. Amen

 NOTES:

JUNE 5TH

Nature's helicopter

JUNE 6TH

'When God measures a person, God puts the tape around the heart instead of the waist.'
~Author Unknown

We all know that there is fixation today about trying to have the correct weight. Glossy magazines, advertising and clever marketing give the impression that we have to be slim. Thankfully God uses different standards. God always looks within to measure the worth of a person.

It is inside that we always find the real person. In our hearts or in our soul there is much love, care, kindness, compassion, healing, character and spirit. In some people it bubbles over and in others they are sometimes slow to recognise all of this within. God is never slow in seeing all of this. God's daily mission is to help nurture so many positive and beautiful qualities within each of us. Too often we are measuring in the wrong place.

 NOTES

Inviting walkway at Blarney, Co. Cork

JUNE 7TH

There's a story told about a frog that fell into a deep rut in a farm laneway. A couple of days later he was still there. Frog friends found him and urged him to get out of his predicament. The frog made a few feeble efforts but remained stuck below in the rut. For the next few days his friends encouraged him to try harder but they finally gave up and went back to their pond. The next day the frog was seen sunning himself along the shore of the pond. 'How did you get out of that rut?' his friends asked. 'Well as you know' said the frog 'I couldn't. But then a tractor came along the laneway and I had no choice but to jump.'

Every one of us has the potential to do so much more, if we only believed in ourselves.

 NOTES:

JUNE 7TH

A Year in Reflection

Pretty bridesmaids and sisters Triona and Maria Jump at Gougane Barra, West Cork

JUNE 8TH

'The easiest thing to be in the world is you. The most difficult thing to be is what other people want you to be.'
~Leo Buscaglia

A constant challenge in life is to be the person God created us to be. We are all gifted and unique. We work best when we do what we're good at and when we do things we enjoy. Unfortunately our world and other people have different expectations of us. They sometimes want to fit us into a box where we simply won't fit. We can't do things we're not good at. We can't be somebody else. Each day God simply wants you to be you. Nothing more and nothing less.

 NOTES

Ballingeary, West Cork, looking its best on a summer's day

JUNE 9TH

'We are not primarily put on this earth to see through one another,
but to see one another through.'
~Peter Vries

No one person can journey on their own or think they can manage a solo run through life. We need support, direction, advice and encouragement. Even with the best of supports around us, life can still be so challenging. Throughout scripture there are many examples of Jesus journeying with people who needed a boost in their lives. Others walked past these people but not Jesus. Is there someone in my life that needs a boost? Can I help someone through this day? The simplest of thoughts and actions on our part can be such a boost to someone else.

 NOTES:

Pilgrims from Ballyvolane/Dublin Hill at Lourdes, France

JUNE 10TH

'We must know people, like them, enjoy them, make friends with them, take trouble for them, before it may ever be right to "speak" to them about spiritual matters.
~Samuel Shoemaker

A community is one where faith thrives, grows and blossoms. In our modern world, community is most at risk from increasing individualism and isolation. All the modern gadgets in the world are vainly trying to help us cope with a lack of community. Spirituality can only take root when there is a sense of community. It can never operate in a vacuum. If there is no community it's all just lip service, shallow and even false. We can't wave a magic wand and hope for instant community, where there is a sense of belonging, friendship and genuine care. But we can do our bit to be more community conscious no matter how small. It can only happen when we realise that every single one of us has a key part to play.

 NOTES

A fine head of cabbage at Tooreenbawn, Millstreet

JUNE 11TH

*'The person who takes a stand is often wrong but those
who fail to take a stand are always wrong.'*
~Author Unknown

There are many issues and situations in life when we need to take a
stand. It is good to declare what we believe in and what we think is right.
We get it right a fair bit of the time but we can also get it so wrong. A
big mistake is thinking others should see our way too. They are fully
entitled to their opinion, position or stand just as you are to yours. But if
we are vague and insincere about issues then we have failed. Our
Gospels challenge us to take a stand in all aspects of life, truth, justice,
faith, peace, fairness, honesty and so on. Trying to get it right with many
of these is indeed challenging but not to try is to fail.

 NOTES:

Boats returning from Skellig Rocks, Co. Kerry

JUNE 12TH

'The only person who behaves sensibly is my tailor. He takes a new measurement every time he sees me. All the rest go on with their old measurements.'
~George Bernard Shaw

We often stick with the old and what seems safe and reliable. This is good and important on occasions but it is also good to try new things in life. Our outlook in life changes as time passes. Every day we adapt to changes all around us. Life moulds us and shapes us. What was once important to us, may now no longer be so. Our Gospels encourage us to be open to life and especially all that is refreshing and life giving in our own lives. To be open to what's new can be risky but always challenging, fulfilling and a great place to be.

 NOTES

Harry Deane's is colourful and eye catching in Drimoleague, West Cork

JUNE 13TH

'Some people are like a wheelbarrow. They go no further than they are pushed.'
~Author Unknown

Only we can honestly answer whether we fall into this category or not. Do we just do the bare essentials or are we willing to do the extra bit. In our Gospels we are encouraged to go the extra mile, to go out of our way in making a difference to someone else and to seize the initiative when no one else will. This does not mean that we are pushed to levels that are uncomfortable or outside what we can do. But we are encouraged to push further than what's needed. It's the extra little bit which can make an extraordinary difference to somebody else. Surely we can't allow our lives to fall into the category of a humble wheelbarrow.

NOTES:

A butterfly is busy at work in the gardens at Tooreenbawn, Millstreet

JUNE 14TH

'I lift my eyes to the hills and where does my help come? My help comes from the Lord.'
~Psalm 121

In a radio competition a prize was offered to whoever could suggest the most descriptive phrase in the English language. The prize winner was 'over the hills and far away'. It also describes all our own journeys too through life. We climb many hills and just as we get over one, another opens out in front of us. We're all on different journeys, we've all got different stories to tell, we've all got different things going on in our lives and we're all on a destination somewhere ahead. Very few can reach such a destination on their own. We are reminded that God is with us and helping us to reach our own destinations in life.

 NOTES

Boats tied up near Ross Castle, Killarney, Co. Kerry

JUNE 15TH

The search for someone to blame is always successful.
~H. Robert

It is easy to blame other people. We're like the small boy who was standing on the cat's tail. His mother hearing the terrible commotion called from the adjoining room, "Tommy stop pulling the cat's tail." "I'm not pulling the cats tail" said Tommy. "I'm just standing on it. He's the one that's doing the pulling!" We have all been there at some stage. It's almost an inbuilt instinct to lay the blame on somebody else. Sometimes we are very hard on ourselves, blaming ourselves for something that was completely outside our control. This presents us with two challenges, to avoid blaming others as best we can and especially to avoid self blame. We ask the Lord for the strength to move on when we genuinely have made a mistake.

 NOTES:

Summer promise at Fitzgerald's Park, Cork

JUNE 16TH

'There are no shortcuts to any place worth going.'
~Beverly Sills

Shortcuts are becoming more attractive because they can generate more time. The fact that there doesn't seem to be enough time these days means that shortcuts are tempting. But not all short cuts are going to work. Any shortcut that sacrifices values such as honesty, respect and the good name of a person is going to fail. The longer road may seem unattractive at times but it has been tested and tried with all of life's experiences. Values such as humility, respect, honesty, simplicity, gentleness and peace are certainly places worth going to. At times they seem to be almost an endangered species. They may not have any value in terms of money but in God's eyes they have infinite value.

 NOTES

The Sullane river gently flows under the bridge at Macroom, Co. Cork

JUNE 17TH

'Better bend than break.'
~Scottish Proverb

All engineering projects, no matter how small or big have to allow for give. Bridges, walls and steel structures all need room to expand with rising temperatures. Not to allow for such expansion will ultimately lead to the collapse of what was built. There are many situations in our lives where we also need to give and take. We sometimes would like to have done it our way but sometimes the best approach is to allow someone else their say and their opinion. In our Gospels Jesus was always flexible, allowing people to have their say and their opinion.

We don't have to agree with everything we hear. But a bit of give and take is so much better than a break and ending up with nothing at all.

 NOTES:

Sunrise in West Cork at Union Hall

JUNE 18TH

'Where ever you go, no matter what the weather, always bring your own sunshine.'
~Anthony Angelo

Sunshine always lifts the spirits and it's easy to see it when we get a few sunny days together. It puts everyone in great form and everyone is determined to make the most of it when it comes. It's up to us too to make the most of our own sunshine and what we can give to others. Like life, the weather may be unpredictable, but we should always bring our own unique sunshine with us wherever we go. Our sunshine, our words, our smile, our presence, our prayers can and do make the world of a difference. It would be a shame if we undervalued the difference we make.

NOTES

Silhouette of a swan and her cygnets at Rosscarbery, Co. Cork

JUNE 19TH

'You can catch more flies with a spoonful of honey than with a barrel full of vinegar.'
~St. Francis DeSales

There are a many people who could be compared to a barrel full of vinegar. They hold onto bitterness, resentments, hurts, grudges and much more. Vinegar has its own purposes but nothing compared to the sweetness and value of honey. A spoonful of honey goes a long way, full of goodness, quality and taste. Like honey, a kind word spoken and genuine warmth and care do make all the difference. In God's eyes the smallest gesture done out of love and kindness is far better than a whole lot of things done without meaning. It is easy to spot the difference between vinegar and honey. It is easy to spot the difference between someone who is shallow and someone with backbone/convictions. Which side am I?

 NOTES:

A Year in Reflection

Six spotted Burnett moth at Robert's Cove, near Carrigaline, Co. Cork

JUNE 20TH

'Do not spoil what you have, by desiring what you have not. Remember that what you now have, was once among the things you only hoped for.'
~Epicurus (Greek Philosopher)

It is easy to desire and look for more. Clever and targeted advertising makes us desire what we think we need. What we think we need is often what we don't need at all. Don't feel guilty that it's just you. We've all been caught by clever advertising. We have more than enough all around us to get on with life. God calls us to do our best with what we have, without excesses. Drawing the line between what is necessary and what is excessive is never easy. Our Gospels draw that line very clearly. Where do we draw the line?

 NOTES

Scenic views on the Ring of Kerry near Waterville, Co. Kerry

JUNE 21ST

'Summer is the season when nature comes into its fullness.'
~Angeles Arrien

Today we celebrate mid summers day and hopefully no rain clouds will dampen the possibility of maximum daylight. The long days of summer encourage anything with enough moisture to stretch towards the sun. Summer is always a season of ripening and abundance. During the coming months many will take a well deserved holiday. It is a time of playfulness and leisure. It is a time to relax and unwind. Our inner spiritual lives also live the season of summer. A deeper spiritual life depends on light and growth. If summer is all about ripening and abundance, then God also wants our potential to ripen. God also wants to extend an abundance of blessings on us. Today we are especially open to such blessings.

 NOTES:

Cuddles with her kitten Patch at Carbery Court, Rosscarbery, Co. Cork

JUNE 22ND

Late one night a man called Percy Shaw was driving through a dangerous run of bends. Rain was falling, visibility wasn't great and suddenly the light from his lights was reflected back from a cat sitting in front of him. Behind the cat was a steep cliff fall. The reflection from the cat's eyes saved him from certain death.

He then spent a full year wondering how he could help others from what happened to him. Using little prisms and mirrors made of aluminium he made the first cats eyes for road use back in 1934. Today there are millions of them to be found on roads all over the world. The image of the cat's eyes can remind us that we too can reflect God's love, care and compassion into the darkest corners of our lives and into the lives of others. Too often we feel we are brave enough on our own. But like cat's eyes on the road we all need God's guidance and reassurance in our lives every day.

 NOTES

Bonfire night in Ballyvolane, Cork

JUNE 23RD

The only survivor of a shipwreck got washed up on a small, uninhabited island. He prayed feverishly for God to rescue him and every day he scanned the horizon for help, but none was forthcoming. Exhausted, he eventually managed to build a hut of driftwood to protect him from the elements. But then one day, after scavenging for food, he arrived home to find his hut in flames, the smoke rolling up to the sky. The worst had happened, everything was lost. He was stung with grief and anger. "God how could you do this to me?" he cried. In a short time he was surprised to hear the sound of a ship approaching the island. It had come to rescue him. "How did you know I was here?" asked the weary man. "We saw your smoke signal," they replied.

When the tough gets going, it is easy to give up. But God is at work in our lives, even when all seems lost.

 NOTES:

St. John's Feast day is marked with Mass at St. John's Well, Mushera, near Millstreet, Co. Cork

JUNE 24TH

'With our faith we are consistently consistent in an unconsistent world.'
~Author Unknown

Today we celebrate the feast of John the Baptist. He was a celebrity in his own way. Thousands flocked to hear him and be baptised by him. But John was not interested in fame. He never wanted to draw attention to himself. He wanted to draw attention only to Jesus. Sometimes we hang our heads and often we're not proud of what we believe in. It's almost as if it is unfashionable and a bit embarrassing to say we believe. John was the exact opposite. He had no reservations and no inhibitions in proclaiming that he was proud to be a follower of Jesus. We too are called to hold our heads up. We are called to be proud of what we believe and to be grateful that we have indeed something to build our lives on.

NOTES

Organic garden at Tooreenbawn, Millstreet, Co. Cork

JUNE 25TH

'The greatest mistake anyone can ever make is to be afraid of making one.'
~Elbert Hubbard

A railway conductor began collecting tickets one morning but discovered that the first passenger had the wrong ticket. "I'm sorry, sir" said the conductor, "but you're on the wrong train. You will have to change trains at the next station." He collected several more tickets and found that these passengers were also carrying the wrong tickets. It seemed strange that so many should have made the same mistake. Then he discovered the truth. He, the conductor, was on the wrong train! We've all been there at some stage. Every mistake made we need to put behind us, because it will only have control over us if we don't. We ask God to give us the strength to move on from mistakes made.

 NOTES:

Cork football team celebrate Munster final day at Pàirc Uì Chaoimh, Cork

JUNE 26TH

'My grandfather told me that there are two kinds of people, those who do the work and those who take the credit. He told me to try to be in the first group where there would be less competition.'
~Indira Gandhi

Which group am I in? It is always tempting to step in and take the credit for work done. Much more important is the work we do ourselves. Sometimes it may be ordinary and mundane. Sometimes it may require hard work and sometimes it is done quietly and without fuss. The same goes with God's work. We are all called to work in the vineyard and do our bit to make God's presence in our world alive, active and relevant. Some may leave it to others and try to take all the credit. But at the end of the day it is God who ultimately knows the work we do, the sacrifices, the efforts and the commitments we make. God never forgets and will always give us the credit.

NOTES

In For The Kill: A spider works hard underneath a fly stuck in its web at Altamount, Millstreet, Co. Cork

JUNE 27TH

'Oh, I've had my moments and if I had to do it all over again, I'd have more of them. In fact, I'd try to have nothing else. Just moments, one after another, instead of living so many years ahead of each day.'
~Nadine Stair on her 85th birthday

There is nothing like the wisdom and advice of an older person. They have been there, they have lived life to the full, they have learned from mistakes made. They have experienced many ups and downs, sorrow and joy. They have journeyed through sweeping changes and transition. They have put their trust in lasting values, a deep faith and strong foundations. As a society we are the biggest losers if we don't listen to their many gems of insight and advice. But in the frantic pace of modern life they are often forgotten. Is there an older person living near me? Can I make contact, offer help or stop for a chat? Better again can I make time to listen to all their wisdom.

NOTES:

Green barley matures slowly but steadily at Dublin Hill, Cork

JUNE 28TH

'For it is when I am weak that I am strong.'
~St Paul

Someone put it very well whey they said, 'I never knew I could until I was told I couldn't.' We all can recall moments when we were told we couldn't do something. Sometimes this was for our own good but on other occasions people underestimated our ability. They thought that we hadn't the brains, or the talent or the guts to go and do something, which we knew in our heart we could do. Thankfully many have gone on to do what they were told they couldn't. For many it has also opened up more gateways and more opportunities. St. Paul also says that even if we have weaknesses, these should always be used as stepping stones and never obstacles. We ask the Lord to help us in all that we can and cannot do.

 NOTES

JUNE 28TH

A butterfly flutters up to its destination at Sugar Hill, Bantry, Co. Cork

June 29th

'Earth provides enough to satisfy the need of every person but not the greed of everyone.'
~Mahatma Gandhi

It is well known that there is enough to go around but wealth and greed mean that the cake is not evenly cut. A good healthy spiritual life always insists on an even cut of the cake. In our Gospel Jesus says it's worth everything we have, our possessions, our efforts, our time and our energy. A healthy spiritual life splits the cake evenly, between work, rest, play and making time to nurture the spiritual. Getting this balance is always a key to happiness. Wealth alone is never a guarantee to inner happiness. Happiness is like a butterfly, the more we chase it, the more it eludes us. But if we turn our attention to God, it comes and softly sits on our shoulder.

Notes:

A Year in Reflection

An orange dusk skyline at Eagle Point, Ballylickey, West Cork

JUNE 30TH

'We're so busy watching out for what's just ahead of us that we don't take time to enjoy where we are.'

~Bill Waterson

Everyone seems to be busy these days. It is a part of modern life and everyone is trying to keep up with the hectic pace of life. It can leave us exhausted at times and often it means that we don't enjoy the present moment or that we don't enjoy all that's around us. This is not a new phenomenon. Jesus took his closest friends away from the crowds too. The crowds were demanding and time out is a part of the Gospel stories. We are about to enter July and August when traditionally people take their holidays. Hopefully our holidays will help us to unwind, relax and do things we normally don't get a chance to do. Even if I'm not on holidays, can I take some time today to enjoy what's good in my life?

 NOTES

JULY

Two young swallows relaxing at Tooreenbawn, Millstreet, Co.Cork

JULY 1ST

'When it comes to peers, don't bow to peer pressure. Make up your own mind.'
~DJ Carey

There are many pressures out there today. Pressures put on us at work, pressures at home, pressures of deadlines, pressures of balancing finances, pressures of sport, pressures of advertising and so on. Sometimes we're put under pressure to go with the flow and to be cool. It can be subtle and gentle while on other occasions it can be strong and powerful. Even Jesus himself was put under pressure. The Pharisees and the Scribes were experts at asking awkward questions. But Jesus was always firm, calm and totally focussed on being himself. We too need to be calm and focussed when others put pressure on us. We need to be confident in ourselves and in our own ability. We ask the Lord for the courage to be strong when it's so much easier to go with the flow.

NOTES:

Sailing lessons at Adrigole West Cork

JULY 2ND

'The most important thing in life, is to learn how to give out love and to let it come in.'
~M Schwartz

We often hear that God loves each of us. It is the foundation stone on which our faith is built. But we have little chance of experiencing God's love for us unless we ourselves can first give love and receive it. It is sad today that many feel unloved and many who are made to feel undervalued and worthless. When someone is hurt and betrayed it is easy to shut out everything including love. God calls each of us to continue giving and sharing love with others. We may not realise if, but our efforts, our little chink of love and light, can give someone else great hope. It would be a great pity and loss if we leave it to someone else.

 NOTES

Cows grazing near Dunmanway, Co.Cork

July 3rd

'You can do anything if you have enthusiasm. Enthusiasm is the yeast that makes your hopes rise to the stars. Enthusiasm is the spark in your eye, the swing in your gait, the irresistible surge of your will and the energy to execute your ideas.'
~Henry Ford

We all need a boost in our lives from time to time. Good news in our community, our family or in our own personal life is always welcome. It's hard to be enthusiastic every single day, but without it we are lost. Some people seem to have a deep reserve of enthusiasm and hope. A closer look and inspection will show that they often have a deep faith which brings meaning to their lives. Their faith is connected to their everyday lives and not just the externals. Such important roots are the generators of enthusiasm and energy. We pray today for enthusiasm, hope and energy in all we do.

NOTES:

Fresh strawberries at Casserres, north of Barcelona, Spain

JULY 4TH

'You have made us for yourself Lord and our hearts are restless until they rest in you.'
~St. Augustine

We often say 'inside out'. We know someone or someplace inside out. In sport the winning team will often have done their homework on the other team. This will include getting to know the opposition inside out. God also knows us inside out and the darkest of our stories is never too dark for God. The biggest stumbling block for people getting to know God is that they feel God wouldn't be interested. Many feel that their darker stories are a hindrance to even begin getting to know God.

This is a pity because God is always interested in us. Our hearts will always be restless until they rest in God. Nothing should be a hindrance or a block for us in getting to know God.

NOTES

Tranquil lake at Millstreet Country Park, Co. Cork

July 5th

'All is not lost until all is totally lost.'
~Author Unknown

It is good to cling to hope even it's only a little chink of light. Some people throw the towel in, while others refuse to give up until every opportunity is explored and tried. Our belief in a loving God helps us to realise that all is not lost. From a faith perspective there is always the possibility of something happening. Getting totally lost thankfully is rare. A strong inner belief will always quietly tell us that we are not lost. Despite knocks, setbacks and disappointments in life we can still be positive and hope for the best. When someone says to us, "you're wasting your time" or "you haven't a hope", we need to be strong.

A comment like that should be the inspiration to believe that all is not lost. We pray today for the strength and guidance to get through each day when all seems lost.

Notes:

A Year in Reflection

A summers evening over Bantry Bay, Co. Cork

JULY 6TH

'How can you expect God to speak in that gentle and inward voice which melts the soul, when you are making so much noise yourself? Be silent and God will speak again.'
~Francois Fenelon

We live in a noisy world. It is so noisy that we have grown accustomed to it. If there isn't noise we are uncomfortable. Every shop, restaurant, hotel and club has music on in the background. At home we have the radio going, televisions on in different rooms and ipod headphones stuck in our ears. All of these are fine in their own way, but they all sacrifice silence. If we can make a few moments of silence in our life each day, we are giving ourselves a great gift. Not only will it help us to relax and unwind briefly, but it is also the best time for God to speak in that gentle and inward voice.

 NOTES

Cattle cooling down in the river Lee near Inchigeela, Co. Cork

JULY 7TH

'God has given us two hands, one to receive with and the other to give with. We are not made cisterns for hoarding, we are channels made for sharing.
~Billy Graham.

If we constantly receive and give nothing we become totally selfish and self centred. We have grown used to the good times with much more money in circulation than ever before. As a result we have grown used to receiving. This is good and important, but if we forget to give something back, the focus is only on ourselves. God has made us to share, especially our time, our gifts and talents, our resources and so on. To hoard any of these is contrary to the gospel message. A person who shares usually gets back far more than they ever gave in the first place.

 NOTES:

A Year in Reflection

Colourful bridge at Belgooly, Co. Cork

JULY 8TH

A group of students were asked what they thought were the present 'Seven Wonders of the World'. Though there were some disagreements, the following received the most votes.

(1) Egypt's Great Pyramids (2) Taj Mahal (3) Grand Canyon
(4) Panama Canal (5) Empire State Building (6) St.Peter's Basilica
(7) China's Great Wall.

While collecting the votes, the teacher noted that one student had not yet finished her paper yet. So she asked the girl if she was having trouble with her list. The girl replied, "Yes a little.

I couldn't make up my mind there were so many." "Tell us what you have and perhaps we might help" said the teacher. Here was her list:

(1) to see (2) to hear (3) to touch (4) our health (5) to feel
(6) to laugh (7) to love.

The room was so quiet there wasn't a word. What we take for granted is indeed the most important of all.

NOTES

A bumble bee landing on a Lupen flower for more pollen.

JULY 9TH

*'Any person who knows all the answers most likely misunderstood
the questions in the first place.'*
~Author Unknown

It would be great if we had all the answers. Every single one of us has so
many unanswered questions. Life can be so unpredictable, unfair and
cruel at times. What did I do to deserve this? Why me? Why not
somebody else? Why now? It's easy to blame somebody else or to
blame God. This is understandable. It becomes unhealthy when we hold
onto blame and never move on with our lives. In our Gospels Jesus never
claimed to have all the answers. Even up on the cross his last few words
were "My God, why have you forsaken me". The invitation is to live the
questions. We pray for the strength to live with our questions and the
strength to walk forward with our lives, even if it's only small faltering steps.

 NOTES:

Brandon Creek facing the Atlantic Ocean, West Kerry

July 10th

Margo asked what her friend's two new dogs were named. Her friend replied that one was named Rolex and one was named Timex. "I've never heard of anyone naming their dogs like that", said Margo.
"But why not", said her friend, "they're watch dogs!!"

Whatever about having a watch dog around us, we are called to be watchful and alert. We are called to be alert to those who need a little lift and boost around us. We think especially of anyone who is bereaved, a relationship that is struggling or broken, an older person living on their own, someone in or just out of hospital. We are not asked to work a miracle or do something big. But a phone call, text or a visit from us can be a major boost to somebody else. What we might see as insignificant can be quite significant to someone else.

 Notes

Colourful Astible at Millstreet Country Park, Co. Cork

JULY 11TH

'My heart is as big as the world.'
~Therese Coudrec

We often say in sport how a particular team plays with great heart and determination. Despite game plans not working out or the opposition faring better, a team can dig in and grind out a result. The same goes with us too. A person who is open to everything in life with great heart usually does very well. Such a person is full of love and makes sure to share it with others. It happens naturally and without fuss. Someone who is cold in their approach to life and who calculate love in terms of cost to themselves will always be catching up. We pray today for a big heart that is open to love, learning, challenges and new possibilities in life.

 NOTES:

JULY 11TH

Taking the horses for water at Cahermee fair, Buttevant, Co. Cork

JULY 12TH

'Stay committed to your decisions but stay flexible in your approach.'
~Tom Robbins

When it comes to deciding whether or not to do something we have three choices: do it, delegate it or ditch it. But we can also delay the decision as well. Sometimes it is good to seize the moment and go for it. But sometimes to delay a decision can be good and positive. In our scriptures Jesus warned about making rash decisions. In the parable of the wheat and weeds, he cautioned against pulling out all the weeds. In doing so, the good wheat could be pulled out as well. He urged them to wait until the harvest and then do the dividing. On our daily journey, we will sometimes have to do it, delegate or ditch it. But we will need at times, to delay, reflect and take our time on some decisions. It is all about finding the right balance.

 NOTES

Reflective waters near the Dunkettle roundabout, Cork

JULY 13TH

'When criticising someone, you might want to consider this. First offer a word of praise and appreciation. Remember the barber always lathers the customer before applying the razor.'
~Author Unknown

It is sometimes good to challenge and criticise someone. We all need it from time to time and we can use it in a positive way. However criticism simply for the sake of it or as a way of knocking someone is an entirely different matter. There are enough people trying to knock others without us adding to it. People never react in the same way to criticism, but always react in the same positive way to praise and appreciation. We ask God to help us to be open to honest criticism, but importantly not to forget those words of praise and appreciation too.

 NOTES:

Red Lucifer laden with raindrops at Tooreenbawn, Millstreet, Co. Cork

JULY 14TH

'When fate shuts a door, come in through the window.'
~Author Unknown

Sometimes life shuts a door on us and on occasions slams it in our face. We've all had some experience of this and perhaps more often than we would have liked. But the unexpected and the unannounced can be a starting point. We have two options, walk away or try and do something about it. We may have to readjust and adapt, but we certainly can pick up the pieces in our lives again and move forward. This is the heart of the Christian message and nothing can erase this hope. What we need more and more today is the ability to cope and adapt to changing circumstances. We ask God today for strength and especially courage, to help us pick up the pieces and find another way forward.

 NOTES

A seal with its young pup on rocks near Ballylickey, West Cork

July 15th

'Give thanks always and for everything'
~St Paul's letter to the Ephesians

If someone were to give you a dish of sand mixed with iron filings to separate, what would you do? To do it by hand would be nearly impossible and very frustrating. But to pull a magnet through the sand transforms the situation. The magnet will pull all the iron filings from the sand to the magnet. The ungrateful person is like our fingers combing the sand. Such a person finds nothing in life to be thankful for. The grateful person is like the magnet sweeping through the sand. They will be grateful for so many little blessings that others may not even see. Little blessings always attract other blessings. Today we thank God for all those blessings in our own lives.

 NOTES:

A Year in Reflection

'When it rains it pours!' at Courtmacsherry, Co. Cork

JULY 16TH

*'Unrealistic expectations are often our downfall. There is no such thing as "Happy Ever After". Learn
and accept that and you'll be....happy ever after.'*
~Paul Brady

We are often hardest on ourselves. We sometimes think we can do
everything. We have unrealistic expectations of ourselves. It's best to
leave Superman and Superwoman to the cinemas. Much more
important is to work within our own abilities and our own limitations. In our
Gospels, Jesus never put anyone under unrealistic expectations. He
always encouraged people and gave them the freedom to express
themselves, to be positive and to work to their own abilities. It's a good
example for us to follow too. The invitation is to try and not be too hard
on ourselves. Once we are aware of our limitations, many more different
things become possible.

 NOTES

'My resting place' at Tooreenbawn, Millstreet, Co. Cork

JULY 17TH

'Some people see things as they are and say 'Why'.
I dream things that never were and say 'Why not?'
~George Bernard Shaw

There are always different ways of seeing things in life.

We are either optimistic or pessimistic or somewhere in between. The constant message from our Gospels is that there is always a bigger picture. If we take one event in isolation it can give a distorted view. It is easy then to ask 'why.' But if we take the bigger picture, if we see life from experience, from a faith point of view, from the foundation of good sound values, then life can be viewed with some optimism. When others say 'why', we are in a better position to try and live with the 'why.'

NOTES:

A Year in Reflection

'Hare In Prayer' on the slopes of Mushera mountain, near Millstreet

JULY 18TH

But the Lord answered: "Martha, Martha, you worry and fret about so many things, and yet few are needed, indeed only one. It is Mary who has chosen the better part, it is not to be taken from her.
~Luke 10:40-42

The story of Martha and Mary is one of the better known Gospel stories. Martha and Mary were both good people and dear friends of Jesus. It was Martha who invited Jesus, but it was Mary who made him feel at home. It was Mary who understood that there is more to friendship than just doing things for someone else. Mary was in touch with the need of people to be accepted for who they are, to share their fears and anxieties and their hopes and joys with someone else. All of us have that need. But not all of us meet that need. Mary did so particularly well. Trying to get the balance between Martha and Mary is the invitation. The rewards are great if we can try to get close.

NOTES

'Playtime' at Tooreenbawn, Millstreet, Co. Cork

JULY 19TH

'If people were meant to pop out of bed, we'd all sleep in toasters.
~Author unknown

Few people can jump out of bed any morning. Some love the mornings, while many more are simply slow starters. But whatever form we are in the morning, we can give each day the best possible start by thanking God for the chance to journey through it. We can ask for God's blessings and direction even as we reach for the snooze button! It may only take a few moments, but if this little prayer doesn't happen at the start of the day, it seldom happens later in the day.

 NOTES:

A water lily on Garnish Island, West Cork

JULY 20TH

'Go and do the same yourself'
~Luke 10:37

The story of the Good Samaritan is probably the most famous in our gospels. It all stemmed from the question, who is our neighbour?

The Jews and Samaritans just didn't get on because of race, political and religious differences. The Samaritan certainly would not have been considered as a neighbour. Yet Jesus says he is. The words of Jesus 'to go and do likewise' was a date to be remembered in the history of humanity. He was saying what no other religion in history ever said, that everyone in the world without exception, is our neighbour. We can go the easy route, of praising the Good Samaritan and saying well done for all he did. The real challenge is for us to do the same and be a Good Samaritan in someone else's life.

 NOTES

Churning up the mud at the Courtmacsherry Strand Races, Co. Cork

JULY 21ST

'Believe while others are doubting.'
~William Ward

Sport penetrates every county, parish and community. Each week so many different games are taking place. Not every team of course can win, but there will always be a trend and some teams just seem to have everything. It is all about their self belief, that they can and will win. If only some of that self belief could rub off on us. If we could just believe even a little more, in our own unique abilities. We may be impatient, but God is so patient with us. Even when we put in seemingly poor performances God always trusts and knows that we have it in us to do better. The biggest obstacle is our huge inability at times, to believe that we have what it takes to do it. We may doubt, but never God!

 NOTES:

Bryon Cooper unsaddling after a race

JULY 22ND

'You don't get ulcers from what you eat. You get them from what's eating you.'
~Vicky Braum

We all have something we're not happy about, something that just won't go away.   Very simply it's eating at us and is doing us no good whatsoever. We may be angry or hurt over something said or done to us. Our lives are complex and what's eating at us is different for everyone. God doesn't or can't wave a magic wand over us with instant results. But God wants us to take some step forward in resolving our issues.   What is eating at me? Can I do something about it?

✏ **NOTES**

A Year in Reflection

An insect walks on a carpet of purple

July 23rd

'A wise person learns by the experiences of others
An ordinary person learns by his or her own experience.
A fool learns by nobody's experience.'
~Author Unknown

We are shaped by our experiences each day. If we are open to learning each day we can benefit greatly from the experiences of other people and benefit greatly from our own experiences too. These will include mistakes made and it's up to us to move on from them. The biggest mistake we could make is to think that we know it all and that we are better than everyone else. In our Gospels Jesus calls such people 'fools'. We can look back on this day and learn from all our experiences.

 Notes:

A goose keeping a close eye on proceedings on a farmyard in the Borlin Valley, West Cork

JULY 24TH

'Whoever wants to be first must place themselves last of all and be the servant of all.'
~Mark 9:35

When a flock of geese migrate in a beautiful V formation, there is a secret to their flying. They work together as a team so that they can fly 70% further to where ever they are going. The leading goose cuts through the air resistance, which creates an uplift for the two birds behind. Their wings beating together make it easier for the birds behind and so on through the V formation. Crucially every bird takes its turn as leader. The tired ones move out to the edges of the V for a breather, having played a crucial role, until it's their turn again. We too are called to do our bit, to give what we can and to play our part in making today special, not just for ourselves, but as a part of God's bigger family.

NOTES

A red cone reflecting the sunlight on Garnish island, West Cork

JULY 25TH

'It isn't much good bolting a door with a boiled carrot.'
~Old Proverb

We all look for security and certainty in life. We find this in family, at work, with friends, in leisure and recreation time. But at different times these can prove fragile. This happens especially with an unexpected crisis. We may have thought we were strong, but soon realise that we are indeed vulnerable. We are always encouraged to place our trust and security in God. Unlike a boiled carrot we have something much more reliable and stronger to fall back on. The invitation is to place our trust and hope in our loving God.

 NOTES:

Nora and Con McSweeney with their grandchildren Daniel and Aoife at Aubane, Millstreet, Co. Cork

JULY 26TH

'What children need most are the essentials that grandparents provide in abundance. They give unconditional love, kindness, patience, humour, comfort, lessons in life and most importantly, little treats.'
~Rudolph Giuliani

Today is the feast of Sts Joachim and Anne, parents of Mary and grandparents of Jesus. Some of the most loving and delightful people we've ever known are our grandparents. The grandparents of Jesus no doubt were proud of their active and energetic grandson. Grandparents are such a huge positive influence in the lives of their grandchildren. Grandparents blossom in the role and its no surprise that grandchildren also adore them. If our grandparents are deceased we remember them, if you are a grandparent, well done and keep up the great good work you are doing and to our living grandparents, we just can't thank you enough

NOTES

Pathway through a barley field at Minane Bridge, Co. Cork

JULY 27TH

'You'll never have all the information you need to make a decision. If you did, it would be a foregone conclusion, not a decision.'
~D Mahoney

Every day we make decisions. Some are straightforward and done without much thought. More can be difficult especially when we are pulled in different directions. It is good advice not to rush into any important decision, but there always comes a point when we have to decide. Sometimes our decisions are not always the correct ones, but all we can do is our best and what we think is right at that particular moment. We ask God's guidance and direction with difficult and brave decisions.

 NOTES:

Feeding time on a telephone wire at Tooreenbawn, Millstreet, Co. Cork

JULY 28TH

'In every community there is work to be done.
In every nation, there are wounds to heal.
In every heart, there is the power to do it.'
~M Williamson

We know we can't change the world, but yet each of us can do so much. The amount of work we do isn't important in God's eyes, but our willingness to do what we can with what we have. God isn't expecting us to sort everything out, or solve all the problems in our community. But we have the power within each of us to do something good and positive. It may not be much in our eyes. It may seem insignificant and hardly worth the effort. But to somebody else, it could make all the difference.

NOTES

'Trying to be the winner' at the Killarney Races, Co.Kerry

JULY 29TH

'We will either find a way or make one.'
~Hannibal

It is easy to say that there is no solution to a difficulty or problem. Sometimes the best of plans run aground and get stuck with seemingly no budge whatsoever. But it's up to us to find a way forward and if it's not obvious then to make one. Often the solution is just within our grasp. The scriptures contain many stories of people in difficult situations with little hope of finding a way forward. Yet God gently guides them through the darkness and difficulties and sometimes through great pain. Our journey is also similar. We are invited to place our trust in God who will always help us find a way forward.

 NOTES:

'Triplets' at Fitzgerald's Park, Cork

JULY 30TH

'Experience is the hardest kind of teacher. It gives you the test first and the lesson afterwards.'
~Author Unknown

We know that experience can get us through all aspects of life, through what's certain, but also through the unknown. Experience is often hard earned. It might be a difficult job interview that didn't go well, the game we should have won but threw away, the decision we should have made but didn't. We spend our lives gathering experiences but they all do stand to us. What is our experience of God? For many people it is wide and varied. All our experiences of God are valid and important. The great lesson of life is to feel loved and cherished. This should be the goal of all our experiences, especially that of God.

NOTES

Michéal and Mary Martin with their daughter Léana walking through Courtmacsherry woods, West Cork

JULY 31ST

'Person to person, moment to moment, as we love, we change the world.'
~S. Kaufman

When we look at the world at large we are simply a drop in the ocean, but what an important drop we are. Much of what happens in the world is completely outside our control. We wish, hope and pray for a more peaceful world. Much more important is how we make a difference in the here and now. God's love for us and our love for each other is the energy we need to keep going. We do our best with each moment of every day. Most go well and some are best forgotten. But for the most part, all our good and love-filled moments are doing great good. Our world today is crying out for much more of these moments.

NOTES:

A Year in Reflection

AUGUST

Golden Harvest near Courtmacsherry, West Cork

AUGUST 1ST

'God loves each one of us as if there were only one of us.'
~St. Augustine

Not everyone believes in this whole heartedly. People have been dealt enough setbacks in life to feel that they have been let down by others including God. But at the heart of all scriptures and everything that has been passed down through the generations, is God's unique love for us. In God's eyes we are unique and precious. So much so that we are celebrated and loved every moment of every day. Nothing that we have done or what we are going to do can change this fact. Those who have a low selfesteem of themselves, those who are riddled with guilt and those who feel they have done everything wrong find this hard to believe. But for you to know that today and everyday you are loved like nobody else. Nothing can change this wonderful truth.

 NOTES:

AUGUST 1ST

Benji a King Charles Calavier is all ready for a game of tennis

AUGUST 2ND

'If you don't believe in God, all you have to believe in is decency. Decency is very good. Better decent than indecent. But I don't think it's enough.
~**Harold Macmillan**

A good foundation is essential for everything in life. Anything less and you are always catching up. It is always good to have something to fall back on in life. A belief in a loving God is probably one of the best foundations any of us can have. We may not have all the answers but at the very least we have something to hold onto when all else fails. It is that little something which makes all the difference.

 NOTES

Colourful tractor at Lisslevane, West Cork

AUGUST 3RD

'One fifth of the people are against everything all the time.'
~Robert Kennedy

You can have all your background work done with the best of plans. You can have the best of ideas and there will always be people who are against you. This is not a reflection on yourself or the work you are doing. It's just the way people are. Perhaps if everyone agreed with everything, life would not be as entertaining or as colourful. In our Gospels, Jesus certainly avoided trying to please everyone. He was always honest and upfront in everything he did and said. Some were against him and many more were deeply moved. The message is very simple don't try and please everyone or you will be very disappointed and frustrated.

NOTES:

Cooling down at Kilmorna Heights, Ballyvolane, Cork

AUGUST 4TH

*'If your foot slips, you may recover your balance. But if your tongue slips,
you cannot recall your words.'*
~Martin Vanbee

We've all had moments when we've lost our balance. It might have
been a drink too many, icy footpaths or greasy floors. We do our best to
recover and move on. But not if we have said something that's hurtful,
nasty or unkind. People's feelings are ever so delicate and fragile. It's fine
to speak our mind and say what needs to be said. But there are always
clear boundaries when enough has been said. There is so much hurt and
pain over things said that shouldn't have been said. We can't just seal
our lips but we can try to make an effort to avoid foul and dirty
language. We can also make an effort to use words that encourage and
uplift rather than words which knock and belittle.

 NOTES

A bumble bee busy at work in Fitzgerald's Park, Cork

AUGUST 5TH

'The squeaking wheel doesn't always get the grease. Sometimes it gets replaced.'
~Vic Gold

We live in a disposable world where nearly everything has a short life span. If something breaks down it seems logical to go off and get it fixed. But today it seems that buying it new, is cheaper than going off to get it fixed or replaced. There are parts of all our lives that feel disposable too. We want this problem solved and other things done for us in an instant. Often like a touch of grease, it is a small change that can make all the difference. Facing the problem head on works far better than trying to skirt round it. We pray today for the strength to face whatever needs to be looked at in our own lives.

 NOTES:

Harvest in full swing at Garretstown, Co. Cork

AUGUST 6TH

'The mill cannot grind with water that is past.'
~George Herbert

Today, grain is ground into flour thanks mainly to modern machinery and technology. But for many years mills used huge wooden wheels turned by water. It was an effective system that simply used the power of nature. Water that had been used simply flowed on elsewhere and the system relied on a constant flow of water. There are similarities with our own lives too. We can use the experience of the past to guide us through today. But we can't expect the past to be the energy for today. Today is best lived with what we have around us. We may not have everything we want but we have more than enough to give today our best chance.

NOTES

Night begins to fall over Millstreet, Co. Cork

AUGUST 7TH

'One of the main reasons why people are not doing well is because they keep trying to get through the day. A more worthy challenge is what I can get from this day.'
~Jim Rohn

When we are simply trying to get through the day it usually drags. The day becomes a routine, monotonous and boring. But every day has the potential to be a good day, a day when I can learn something new or do something I didn't do yesterday. Often doing something small well can have a much bigger impact than trying to do everything together.
Lord, I find some days long, doing the same thing each day.
Help me to see each day as a fresh start and a new beginning.
Help me to make the most of today as you have given it to me.

NOTES:

A cow grazes on a cliff face near Clonakilty, West Cork

AUGUST 8TH

'Having the best idea will do you no good unless you act on it. People who want milk shouldn't sit on a stool in the middle of a field hoping that a cow will back up to them.'
~ C Grant

We are all capable of generating ideas. Some we dismiss straight away, some we think about, and more we sit around hoping the idea will kick into action all by itself. Not every idea is going to work out, but it's up to us to try it out. In our Gospels, we see how Jesus had ideas that initially seemed futile and a waste of time. The example of the five loaves and two fish to be divided among 5,000 bordered on the ridiculous. Everyone had more than enough to eat. Any idea of ours that is good always has potential. It can only happen unless we are willing to give it a go.

NOTES

Tranquil Robert's Cove, near Carrigaline, Co.Cork

AUGUST 9TH

'Physical disarray adds to the tensions of life. Clearing out the clutter is an orderly way to calm.'
~Paul Wilson

It is wellknown that clutter, physical disarray and disorganization, can lead to stress and tension. We tend to hoard so many unnecessary bits and pieces. Getting rid of all these can create a new fresh space that is both healthy and life giving. In our Gospels, Jesus lived and travelled light. He also encouraged others to do the same. We are encouraged to make more space for calm and quietness among the clutter of our own lives. It is easy to say we'll do it next week or next month. Today could be a good day to begin the big clean up.

NOTES:

Splash of pink at Tooreenbawn, Millstreet, Co. Cork

AUGUST 10TH

'It is easy to be an angel when nobody ruffles your feathers.'
~Anonymous

It's hard to be angel, because there are few days when our feathers aren't ruffled by people and events happening around us. Sometimes people intentionally annoy us and more times people do things without even realizing how much it annoys us. It often calls for great patience but we all know that there are times when it's not easy. Even Jesus himself got ruffled by other people such as the Scribes and Pharisees who were snobs. They thought they were perfect and that everyone else should be like them. Jesus wasn't long telling them otherwise. It is human and normal to get annoyed and angry with other people. Verbal arguments don't always solve everything and for the most part we do need an endless supply of patience!

 NOTES

Round bales of straw, at Farran, Macroom, Co. Cork

AUGUST 11TH

'No one's around when the work needs to be done,
but everyone shows up when the bread is ready.'
~Author Unknown

Not everyone can appreciate the work and effort that we personally put into different aspects of our daily lives. There is no barometer in measuring the amount of love, care, dedication, sacrifice, courage and determination that many people give each day. There are plenty who will try and take the credit. In God's eyes, the person who quietly works away without making a fuss is indeed a real winner. Perhaps there is someone in our lives too who is doing tremendous work but whom we may be taking very much for granted. It is easy to turn this one around but only if we decide to do something about it.

 NOTES:

Meadow Walk at Millstreet Country Park, Co. Cork

AUGUST 12TH

'Hope makes you reach when you know your arm is too short.
Hope gives you that extra added stretch to reach it after all.'
~Author Unknown

Without hope there is no tomorrow and, without it, today begins to crumble. We all need some hope in our lives. Many of us have been pushed beyond our limits at times. But somewhere from within, we do our best to keep going. In our Gospels, Jesus constantly inspired people and gave each of them renewed hope and life. Seemingly impossible situations were completely turned around. We can never say that we have enough hope. We pray for renewed hope and life, whatever our own situation may be. We pray especially for any person or family whom we know is going through a difficult time. We pray for hope in their lives today.

 NOTES

Why bother with a trailer at Millstreet Horse show!

AUGUST 13TH

'There is no happiness but there are moments of happiness.'
~Spanish Proverb

Everyone longs for happiness. People have always been searching for the right recipe. It didn't start today or yesterday but has been going on for thousands of years. A few things are clear from that length of time. Money can never buy happiness. Happiness is often shortlived. It also needs to be shared. A person who is connected to their faith is often a step ahead in reaching happiness. Our proverb today sums it up best when it tells us that there is no lasting happiness in this world. We are only travelling through. We can ,and will, encounter many moments of happiness on that journey. It is up to us to seize them and to celebrate them. What a shame to miss these moments if our focus is elsewhere.

 NOTES:

'Me Please': A parent swallow arrives with an insect for one of her enthusiastic offspring at Tooreenbawn, Millstreet

AUGUST 14TH

'Knock the 't' off the 'can't.'
~Samuel Johnson

When we take our eye off what needs to get done or what's important in life, the chances are high that we are missing out on a lot. We need to give that 100% into what needs getting done. This does not mean giving 100% of our time, seven days a week. What it does mean, is that when we do something, no matter how small, it's best to give it our all.

In our Gospels, Jesus constantly encouraged people to do their best, to keep focussed and especially on the really important things in life.

When we find ourselves saying 'I can't', we pray for the encouragement to say 'I can'.

 NOTES

A beautiful stained glass window of Mary at Lourdes, France

AUGUST 15TH

'There is only one path to heaven. On Earth, we call it love.'
~Author Unknown

Today is the feast of the Assumption of Mary into heaven. It is always a turning point in late summer, not just for those getting the Leaving Cert results but also a reminder that the school holidays will soon be winding down as we head for September. At the heart of this feast day is a sense of hope. Mary was taken up into heaven to show the other side of death. Death is always so final, but as believers we believe in eternal life. It's the hinge on which we rest everything. The Assumption of Mary is a reminder that we are merely pilgrims as we journey through this world. What happened to Mary is God's plan for all of us too. Sometimes we need a boost and a reminder that there is a meaningful purpose to life. Today is certainly one of those days.

 NOTES:

Showing off the sheep at Kilgarvan show, Co. Kerry

AUGUST 16TH

'Whoever gossips to you will also gossip of you.'
~Spanish Proverb

They say nothing travels faster than the speed of light but it seems bad news travels just as fast. Gossip thrives on bad news, it thrives on rumours and it thrives on the unknown. So many people have been upset and deeply hurt by gossip. It's bad enough on its own, but when it is fuelled by drink, it becomes a pathetic story. The proverb today sums it up so well. Whoever gives us a juicy bit of gossip, will also gossip of us. Gossip has no boundaries and no conscience. It is also fair to say that we've all been there at some stage. But perhaps today we can ask ourselves honestly if our conversation is honest, helpful and encouraging, or does it thrive on what's trivial, untrue and vague?

NOTES

Stretching towards the sun at Fitzgerald Park, Cork

AUGUST 17TH

'If you pray for another, you will be helped yourself.'
~Yiddish Proverb

Prayer is easier than we think. We say to ourselves that it's too hard and that we don't have the proper time for it. It's so easy to look for excuses. The easiest prayer is to pray for ourselves, praying that we will get through this day as best we can. It is always good to pray for other people too, especially when we may not be able to help them in the way we want. What a great gift to give to someone by saying a little prayer for them. Not only will they benefit, but we too will benefit. Every person who prays always receives blessings. When it rains, it's not just one flower that benefits but every flower. Each prayer, no matter how small or short, is always valued, appreciated and well worth the effort.

 NOTES:

Upside down at Natter Jack's pub, near Castlegregory, Co. Kerry

AUGUST 18TH

'Peace I bequeath to you, my own peace I give you, a peace the world cannot give, this is my gift to you. Do not let your hearts be troubled or afraid.'
~John 14:26-27

Peace has been given many descriptions. It is not just an absence of war, nor is it simple harmony. True peace is not the same as tranquility. Tranquility is external, whereas peace is internal. It is an inner state of calm. Everyone longs for it, few find it fully, and we are reminded that it is a precious gift from God. The invitation is to allow ourselves to be loved and if we love, we will find a greater peace than we ever imagined. For all this to happen, we need to accept ourselves as we are, the ugly and the beautiful in each of our lives, the good and the bad, our strengths and weaknesses. We acknowledge those parts of our lives that are worried or anxious and we pray especially for God's peace and calm.

 NOTES

Lace Cap Hydrangea is a sea of blue at Tooreenbawn, Millstreet

AUGUST 19TH

When Matt Busby (famous manager of Man Utd) died, Denis Law was asked, 'What's your greatest memory of Matt Busby?' He replied; 'His face the night we had won the European Cup.'

Our face has often been described as the window to our soul. It is very important. To remember someone is to remember the face. Our face is capable of so many different expressions. We recognise this with the expressions we use. How often we talk about 'loosing face', 'saving face', 'two faced', 'faceless' and so on. Just as the human face can express so many different things, we often put on a mask disguising how we are feeling. Jesus often looked into the face of those he met. With love and compassion he took down the mask and met that person where they were at. What is my facial expression today and those nearest to me? Am I sensitive to how someone is really feeling?

 NOTES:

Fun at the circus in Bantry, West Cork

AUGUST 20TH

'Every now and then go away, even briefly. Have a little relaxation, for when you come back to your work, your judgment will be surer since to remain constantly at work will cause you to lose power'.
~Leonardo da Vinci

A lot of people are doing their best to make the most of what's left of the summer holidays. Dare we mention the word 'school' at this stage! Any sunny day now entices families to get away to the beach or even to the circus. It is always good to get away from home, break the routine and recharge the batteries. But when the summer break does come to an end, we still need to make time for those little breaks. Time is precious and we are busy with so much. But we are also precious too. Time out, even if it's only very brief, is one of the best investments we can make.

 NOTES

Sailing home at Castlegregory, Co. Kerry

AUGUST 21ST

'Conversation is like a boat - if everybody crowds on the same side, it sinks.
It needs balance to keep it afloat.'
~Marjorie Pither

Mobile phone companies tell us that we, as a nation, love to talk on our phones. We spend more time talking on the phone than any of our European neighbours. We are good at conversation and use it to brighten up every moment and occasion. Sometimes our conversations can be negative or critical of other people. Our conversation can, at times, be juicy gossip and, as a result, puts us and others very much off balance. It is up to us to bring the balance back in. If our conversations tend to be negative and critical, why not try something that is uplifting and more positive. Prayer, no matter what form it takes, is a conversation with God. It can be a great step forward in bringing some overall balance.

 NOTES:

Dandelions flourish at Rathcooney, Co. Cork

AUGUST 22ND

'If dandelions were hard to grow, they would be most welcome on any lawn.'
~Andrew Mason

I can remember in school our science teacher telling us that a weed is a flower in the wrong place. It was a simple explanation but one that I have never forgotten. The weed is also symbolic of those people that we don't like or those people that simply irritate us. These people, like a flower, also have their good qualities. But because we see them as a weed, they tend not to be welcome, in our own gardens. The following prayer might be useful today: 'Lord, its hard to get on with everyone. In fact, at times, it's nearly impossible! When someone is really annoying me, help me to see the flower rather than the weed. This may be difficult right now. But Lord, I do want to give it a go, knowing that there are times too when I'm not always a flower!'

 NOTES

Cliff views near Castletownbere, West Cork

AUGUST 23RD

'The same set of stones may be stumbling blocks or stepping stones, depending on how we use them.'
~Russian Proverb

There are certain aspects of all our lives which overlap. A lot of what overlaps is good and positive. We all have an appreciation of special and significant occasions, like the birth of a baby, a christening, a birthday, an unexpected surprise, a sporting occasion and so much more. Sometimes we also hit difficult patches in our lives. These patches can be obstacles or stepping stones. A lot depends on our attitude and our willingness to see these difficult patches as short term. Jesus constantly encouraged people to change their attitudes. He gave people the self belief that negative life situations should never dominate and are always short term. No situation in life is ever impossible.

NOTES:

Beautiful red rose at Tooreenbawn, Millstreet

AUGUST 24TH

'Do not walk through time without leaving worthy evidence of your passage.'
~Pope John 23rd

All of us are aware just how precious time is. As the 'back to school' promotions hit us in many shops, many people are remarking just how quickly the summer months went. We are encouraged to use our time well and to leave a positive mark in our world each day. No matter how small or trivial this mark may seem to us, it has immense value and potential, especially with God. There may be some who are determined to leave negative marks around us. But these people should not bully us into doing the same. We need to hold our heads up high, be proud of our best efforts and be willing to keep doing our best. We don't have to account for others but we have total control over our mark in this world.

 NOTES

'Pain': The Pro Tour Of Ireland comes up Patrick's Hill, Cork

AUGUST 25TH

'It is only if you have been in the deepest valley, that you can know how magnificent it is to be on the highest mountain.'
~Author Unknown

Life as we know is a journey through joy and pain. Our faith and our belief in a loving God, touches in on both. One can't separate one from the other. We know that the life of Jesus wasn't just all easy or plain sailing. He underwent much pain, hardship and suffering, especially during his last hours. All of this was endured by Jesus, not to become a hero but was done out of pure love for each of us. His journey through the deepest of valleys is a reminder just how in touch the Lord is with our own struggles, hurts and disappointments. God unites all of these, unites all of us together and enables us to move forward out of our deepest valleys with a great sense of hope.

 NOTES:

'Designer Boot' at Glengarrif, West Cork

AUGUST 26TH

'We have what we seek. It is there all the time and if we give it time,
it will make itself known to us.'
~Thomas Merton

New Zealand is famous not just for its rugby but also for its flightless birds. There are more of them in New Zealand than any part of the world, such as the kiwi and the penguin. Scientists tell us that these birds had wings but lost them as they had no use for them. They had no natural predators and food was plentiful. Since there was no reason to fly, they didn't, and through neglect they lost their wings. There are things too in our lives that we can loose through neglect. It might be love, a friendship, a particular gift or talent, our faith and so on. It's easy to drift and easy to loose. God brings to us all we seek in life, especially what really matters. What a shame to loose it by neglecting what has been given to us.

 NOTES

'Best Friends': Trish Macropoulos with 'Ray' are all smiles at the West Cork Equine Centre

AUGUST 27TH

'The human spirit is stronger than anything that can happen to it.'
~George Scott

Most people live on the circumference of life. Our outer world is full of static, clutter and confusion. In a world where nothing seems to stand still, it is often hard to find calm and a sense of peace. Not many move from the chaos of this world into the inner part of each person that we call the soul or spirit. But this sacred place within each person is incredibly strong. It is that place within each of us where the heartbeat of God rests. This is not something scary or weird. It is beautiful, normal and healthy and some just radiate it so naturally. But if we live only on the circumference of life, we can neglect, forget and stifle what is so precious within. Small steps off the hectic pace of the circumference of life could be very worthwhile.

 NOTES:

Clouds Of Dust at a forest rally near Castlemartyr, Co. Cork

AUGUST 28TH

'Blessed is the influence of one true, loving human soul on another'.
~ George Eliot

There can be many different types of influence ranging from weak to strong, and from negative to positive/good. Perhaps we take for granted the influence we have on each other, particularly the good and positive.

No matter how ordinary today may be, you will have a unique influence on someone, perhaps without even knowing it. These are the moments that make every day worthwhile.

Lord, help me to believe in myself and particularly in my own good and positive influence on other people.

 NOTES

Sunset over Kenmare, Co. Kerry

AUGUST 29TH

'If we could all confess our sins to each other we would all laugh at
one another for our lack of originality.'
~Kahil Gibhran

Like a wall, everyone has some fault or crack. Some are small, some large and some have been patched up and still visible. It is similar with our own lives. We all have done some wrong and have let ourselves and others down. Just as a setting sun brings one day to a close, we can also bring to a close those areas of our lives that are best forgotten.

Asking God to forgive us is a great start. Too many feel that God just couldn't forgive them and feel unworthy of forgiveness. Nothing could be further from the truth. God's forgiveness is unlimited with no strings attached. Is there any part of my life that needs forgiveness? Can I bring it to God, experience the healing of God's forgiveness and move on with my life?

 NOTES:

A pine tree with striking red colours on Garnish island, West Cork

AUGUST 30TH

'Never judge a summer resort by its postcards.'
~Author Unknown

It is so easy to be deceived by such postcards. Perfect sunsets, perfect waves, perfect blue skies and perfect sand make sure we get carried away. Travel brochures simply whet our appetite. We go there expecting exactly as it says in the book. It doesn't always quite work out that way. It goes for many things in life. Our expectations can often be built up through glossy advertising. There are subtle pressures to keep up pace with a perfect world. Such a world doesn't exist or never will. It's a pace that can wear out, even the strongest. It is up to us to dictate our own pace through life, not what others think it should be at.

 NOTES

'Maternal Love' An alpaca lovingly watches over her little cria named 'Augusta'

AUGUST 31ST

'People change when they are given hope, when someone believes in them and gives them a task to do. Above all they change when they are loved. They come out of their shells and hidden energies are released in them.'
~Flor McCarthy

If we could only realize the world of a difference our love can make in someone's life. I don't think we fully appreciate our goodness, how much our kindness matters and how our love transforms others. We do it and we simply move on. If we could just know the amount of hidden energies we release in others when we do our bit and our best, we'd be amazed. The hectic pace of life quickly moves us on. But God has actively been involved in that moment and in the next moment we do it again. It would be a great shame to underestimate the great good you are doing. The message is simple today.....keep going and keep it up!

 NOTES:

SEPTEMBER

Golden Gate Bridge, San Francisco, U.S

SEPTEMBER 1ST

'The Lord is my rock, my fortress and my deliverer.'
~ 2 Samuel 22:2

Probably one of the most famous bridges in the world is the Golden Gate Bridge in San Francisco. Although it is built over what is called the 'San Andreas fault', the Golden Gate Bridge is probably the safest place to be during an earthquake. A rock-solid foundation underneath and flexibility above are the reasons why. Careful engineering has designed the bridge to be anchored by two towers sunk deep into the rock beneath and a network of cables overhead, making it so flexible that it can sway 22feet horizontally and 12feet vertically. It can adapt to external changes, wind, storms and even earthquakes. We can also ask ourselves: am I anchored securely? Is God my anchor? Do I have the flexibility necessary to cope with so many changes around me? Am I flexible enough to allow room for God in my life?

NOTES:

Window display in the build-up to the All-Ireland Hurling Final at Kilmorna Heights, Ballyvolane

SEPTEMBER 2ND

'A move from zero to one is the best learning experience.'
~Woody Allen

During the past few days many children began school for the very first time. It was a unique milestone in their young lives and a proud moment for their parents too. Much will be learned during the coming years but always in small steps. The same goes for all of us in life as well. We are all learning more about ourselves each day, learning more about our faith and learning more from those around us.

We adapt to all of life's changing circumstances at our own pace. This can never happen in big sweeping movements. We pray that all of us, no matter what our age, will be open to learning and new possibilities in our lives. Small but significant steps forward are the ones that will bring the greatest return.

 NOTES

Buttercup stands out amongst the heather at Millstreet Country Park, Co. Cork

SEPTEMBER 3RD

'There are as many nights as days and one is just as long as the other in the year's course. Even a happy life cannot be without a measure of darkness. The word 'happy' would lose its meaning if it were not balanced by sadness.'
~Carl Jung

Life is indeed a mixture of happiness and sadness. Nobody has a say in the making up of that mixture. It would seem that some people and some families have more than their share of sadness and troubles.

In our Gospels Jesus never promised to wipe out sadness. It is a part of our journey through this world. But Jesus did promise to make that journey easier and did everything to bring light, hope and healing into whatever form of sadness he came in touch with. We pray for anyone experiencing sadness or going through a difficult patch. We show our support by extending our love and friendship in whatever way we can.

NOTES:

Rebels ready to go in Croke Park for the All-Ireland Hurling Final

SEPTEMBER 4TH

'Discipline begins with small things done daily.'
~Author Unknown

Great sporting teams and sports players have a great discipline in all they do. It doesn't just happen and requires great self-sacrifice, dedication and the willpower to overcome obstacles along the way. The same goes in life too. Hoping for the best or leaving everything to the last minute is bound to let us down at times. Even our spiritual journey can't be left to chance. It's impossible to get close to God if we're only asking for miracles. Getting through life needs discipline and in particular doing the small things as best we can. It's up to us to choose our attitude for any given day. It's up to us to keep the bigger picture always in focus. A great discipline each day is to do what we can and to leave others to worry about what they should be doing.

 NOTES

Splash: A seal hits the water out in Kenmare Bay, Co.Kerry

SEPTEMBER 5TH

'Sometimes it is more important to discover what one cannot do, than what one can do.'
~Lin Yutang

We all have our limitations. It's good to have them because without them we would simply burn out in trying to do everything. Now that the schools have reopened for a new term, there is a sense of everything and everyone getting back to a normal routine again. It is good to re-examine what our plans and hopes are for the coming few months. Sometimes writing them down makes them much clearer. There will be some well within our reach, some beyond our reach and some that we hope might happen. We ask God to give us inspiration, energy and direction in all we hope to do, knowing that we all have our limitations.

NOTES:

Slowly but surely: A ladybird climbs a blade of grass at Tooreenbawn, Millstreet

SEPTEMBER 6TH

'Kind words are jewels that live in the heart and soul and remain as blessed memories years after they have been spoken.'
~Marvea Johnson

If only we could count the number of words we use each day. We'd probably be surprised at the huge number. Here in Cork we love to talk and it just comes naturally! If we were to break that number into two groups, kind words and nasty words, where would the balance swing? Only we can answer that one for ourselves. We should never underestimate the value of a kind word. What a lift it can bring to somebody. There is enough of negative stuff in our world today. It is up to us to bring a little balance in, with words of encouragement and kindness. It doesn't require a huge effort but no money can buy the results.

 NOTES

Blackberries nearly ripe at Eagle Point, Ballylickey, West Cork

SEPTEMBER 7TH

'Terms and conditions apply'.

~Final insert on many of our radio and television advertisements

How often we hear these great offers and promotions. We are led to believe just how lucky we are. But each one finishes with the catchphrase 'terms and conditions apply'. Sometimes they are even apologetic by saying 'only a few terms and conditions apply.'

God's love for us has no terms and conditions. It is totally free, unconditional and there for the taking. Nothing can diminish God's love for us. Nothing will stop God loving us. We don't need money or a bank account. We don't need to have all the answers or we don't have to be saints. God accepts us as we are with no strings attached whatsoever. Can I allow myself to be loved and feel loved by God?

 NOTES:

Holy Trinity: The central yellow and black colours make out the unique shape of the Holy Trinity

SEPTEMBER 8TH

'The Love of God has been poured into our hearts by the Holy Spirit
which has been given to us.'
~St. Paul to the Romans 5:5

I like the word 'poured' in this line from St. Paul. It accurately describes the outpouring of blessings that God always wants to bring to us. The Holy Trinity (Father, Son and Holy Spirit) is sometimes hard to explain. There are things in life that we will never fully understand. We often have honest questions that need honest answers. Unfortunately the answers don't always come even from a faith perspective. Sometimes we have to live the questions and hope that in time we will find the answers. The Holy Trinity is a reminder that despite mystery in life and mystery surrounding God, we should never forget that, God is closer to us than we can possibly imagine.

 NOTES

A crannóg at Millstreet Country Park, Co. Cork

SEPTEMBER 9TH

'Never allow someone to be your priority while allowing yourself to be their option.'
~Author Unknown

It is true that other people can and do take advantage of us. It happens in all walks of life, to people of all different ages and in many different and varied circumstances. Just as an electric current will always take the shortest route possible, there are people out there who will use us as the shortest route possible. Outwardly these people are friendly, warm and appear good intentioned. But it is they themselves who are the priority and not you. Even Jesus met people who appeared nice and well intentioned but were only using him for their own purposes. It is part of life and will always be there. But at the same time it's good for us to know that we are worth so much more than to allow others take advantage of us.

 NOTES:

SEPTEMBER 9TH

Watchful eyes from this owl at Blandford, Dorset, England

SEPTEMBER 10TH

'A wise old owl sat on an oak tree,
The more the owl saw the less it spoke,
The less the owl spoke the more it heard,
Why aren't we like that wise old bird?'
~E Richards (Poet)

It is true that if we spoke less and paused to look all around us we'd be surprised what we might see and hear. It is possible to get so caught up with the immediate that we fail to see the beauty of this day all around us. It's not difficult to make an effort to appreciate more of what's around us. Today is as good a day as any to begin.

 NOTES

Delicacy: The fuschia flower in full bloom on Garnish Island, West Cork

SEPTEMBER 11TH

'The happiest people don't necessarily have the best of everything.
They just make the best of everything.'
~Author Unknown

Clever advertising gets you to think that you need something. Once we have this something then we'll be happy. But once we have that something there is always just one more thing to complete the happiness picture. For many that picture is never complete. Our Gospels remind us that we will get closer to happiness is by making the best of what we've got. It's not just about making the best of physical things but also making the best of our own uniqueness, of our own gifts and talents and making the most of what we can do each day. Our prayer today is for guidance in understanding the difference between having something and making the best of something. There is a world of a difference between the two.

 NOTES:

A Year in Reflection

Thirsty Work: A squirrel enjoying a well-deserved break at Central Park, San Francisco, U.S.

SEPTEMBER 12TH

'A sense of humour doesn't necessarily mean a knack for telling jokes. It means the ability to take some setbacks and still see that the world has not come to an end.'
~Author Unknown

We all experience setbacks. Some are serious, challenging and can knock us right off our track. Other setbacks are much less serious. When these happen we can just readjust and simply move on. But for some these lesser setbacks are as if the world has come to an end.

We hear a litany of complaining and giving out. When such lesser setbacks are put next to other people's real stories and pain, these lesser setbacks fade into total insignificance. Smaller setbacks and knocks are a feature of all our lives. Let's be honest we're luckier than most and we can count our blessings. We pray today for any person or family who really is experiencing those tough and difficult setbacks in life.

 NOTES

Wall Of Death: Riding dangerously in full formation at top speed at the Great Dorset Steam Fair, England

SEPTEMBER 13TH

'Pride comes before a fall'.
~Book of Proverbs 16:18

A frog planned how to get away from the cold winter climate. "I've got a splendid brain. I know what I'll do," he said to himself. Then he approached two geese that soon would start on their migrating journey to a warmer country. "I would like to migrate with you," he said.
"But you can't fly," said the geese. "I know" said the frog "but I have a plan". "You pick up a strong reed, each holding one, end and I'll hold on to it with my mouth." The geese agreed and started their journey. Soon they were passing over a small town and someone cried out, "look, Look. Who could have thought of such a clever idea?" Hearing this, the frog was so full with a sense of pride and importance that he croaked out loud; "I planned it." The frog lost its hold on the reed and the rest is history. Is there a bit of the frog in me at times?

✒NOTES:

A drop of water transforms the beauty of this leaf at Tooreenbawn, Millstreet

SEPTEMBER 14TH

'I can't understand why people are frightened of new ideas.
I'm frightened of the old ones.'
~John Cage

Thankfully new ideas are constantly in the making. It keeps life fresh, active and moving forward. But not everyone is welcoming of an idea or something new. We can be sure we will bury a new idea if we say some of the following: "It will never work." "We've never done it before." "We're doing fine without it." "We can't afford it." "We're not ready for it." "It's not our responsibility." Not every new idea is going to take root but every new idea deserves to be heard and given every chance. In our Gospels Jesus reminds us that the tiniest of all the seeds is a mustard seed. Yet it thrives and grows into something big and special. I can be a constant knocker of potential or I can do my best to encourage every potential no matter how small.

 NOTES

Laneway views at Castletownshend, West Cork

SEPTEMBER 15TH

'Swallow your pride occasionally, it's non fattening!'
~Author Unknown

We sometimes think that we are infallible, that we are always right and that our viewpoint is the only one. But this is not always so. We do on occasions need to swallow our pride and put our hands up and say 'I got this one wrong'. If we can learn from it then we are so much the better from the experience. We're not on our own in admitting failure and we certainly won't be the last. It doesn't mean that we are complete failures but it does mean that a different approach or a different angle would have made all the difference. Can I be strong enough to admit that I got it wrong? We ask God for the strength and courage to try a different approach.

NOTES:

A Year in Reflection

Cobh Co. Cork looking majestic on a September morning.

SEPTEMBER 16TH

'Though our feelings come and go, God's love for us does not.'
~C.S Lewis

A story is told about the late Mother Teresa who was very upset about heavy storms and flooding in Calcutta. She spoke to a priest about her distress and near despair. 'How can I go among all the poor people and talk to them about the love of God?' The priest gave her a profound answer, 'Go among your people, but don't talk to them about the love of God, be the love of God to them.' Our actions often speak louder than words. I can extend God's love into someone's life today and, more often than not, it's the smallest action of love that can have the biggest effect.

✒ NOTES

Unique: The O'Duffy Cup, the Brendan Martin Cup, the Liam MacCarthy Cup and the Eircom League of Ireland Cup could only be reunited in one county.....Cork!!

SEPTEMBER 17TH

'I am thankful to be given the chance to perhaps be in the right place at
the right time and so be a light in life of a few.'
~Roisin Hall

How often have we heard someone say that they were in the wrong place at the wrong time. If only the clock could be turned back to change things but sadly it can't. Just as the clock can't turn back, neither can it be pushed forward and that leaves us with today. This day is made up of many significant moments. Thankfully we can choose to be in the right place at the right time for someone in our lives today. It need not be earth shattering and it need not cost the world. God is often most active and alive in the simplest, down to earth moments of our daily lives. Any gesture done with love means we are always in the right place at the right time.

NOTES:

Harvest threshing at the National Ploughing Championship

SEPTEMBER 18TH

'The best way out of a problem is through it.'
~Old Saying

A story comes to mind about a farmer who ploughed around a large rock in his fields for many years. He had broken many ploughshares in that time. One day after breaking another piece of his plough he decided to finally do something about it. When he put a crowbar under the rock he was surprised that it lifted quite easily. He lamented all the time he lost working around it instead of working with it. Like the farmer we often plough around problems. Often the best way of tackling any problem is to deal with it straight away and straight on. This was the way Jesus dealt with any problem he encountered in our Gospels. We are assured of that same help, too, with whatever our problems may be.

NOTES

A snail takes its time climbing up a leaf at Kilmorna Heights, Ballyvolane

SEPTEMBER 19TH

'Ordinary riches can be stolen, real riches cannot. In your soul are
infinitely precious things that cannot be taken from you.'
~Oscar Wilde

There are many things that can be taken from us in life. Even under lock and key nothing is absolutely safe. But there are many things within each of us that are just so precious. These are special and unique to you. They are in that sacred place called the soul of each person. Your faith may be barely hanging in there, lukewarm or deep rooted. But it can never take from what's special to you. The problem is that so many completely ignore the vast treasures within each of us. Our world may not be the nicest of places at times, but there is such a reserve of deep love in so many people that it can't be ignored. This deep reserve is God's most precious gift to each of us.

 NOTES:

The Evening Echo Women's Mini Marathon in full swing down Monaghan Road, Cork

SEPTEMBER 20TH

An Arabian chief left 17 camels to his 3 sons. The eldest was to get half, the middle son a third and the youngest one ninth. Try as they might they were unable to divide the camels. They went to one of the village elders for help. She thought for a moment and came up with an imaginative solution. She knew you couldn't divide in half an odd number of camels. She offered as a gift her own camel and that when they were all divided she could have what was left over. They agreed. So they divided the eighteen camels. The eldest son got nine. The middle who was to get one third, got six and the youngest who was to get one ninth got two. Now nine plus six plus two equals seventeen, the same number that they were given in the first place. When they had all finished laughing at how simple it all was, they returned the extra camel to the village elder and went off home.

It is easy to get completely immersed in a problem and become blind to other possibilities. We may see no option when in fact with the help of others there may be many options open to us.

✎ NOTES

President Mary McAleese is all smiles at the National Ploughing Championship

SEPTEMBER 21ST

'The measure of love is to love without measure.'
~St. Augustine

We all like to have a sense of how much or how little. Our telephone bills are measured in units, mobile phones in minutes and seconds, petrol and diesel in litres and so on. But how do you measure love?

It is something that is nearly impossible to do. St. Augustine sums it up well by saying the measure of love is to love without measure. This means to love with everything we've got. It's not about being selective or loving when we're in the mood. If we believe God is love and if we believe love is the greatest energy in our world and lives, then nothing can stop its great momentum. Love will always touch the sadness and joys of our world. It knows no boundaries or obstacles. It is our Christian call and indeed our daily challenge to love without measure.

NOTES:

Concentration during the National Ploughing Championship

SEPTEMBER 22ND

'No one who puts their hand to the plough and looks back is fit for the kingdom of God.'
~Luke 9:62

The ploughing championship pulls in over 170,000 people in three days making it one of the biggest rural festivals in Europe. Even back in the time of Jesus ploughing was important. Using the image of the plough, Jesus said the person who is constantly looking back will get nowhere. It's much better to look at where we're going than to see where we've been. Too much time is wasted and lost in looking back. This is especially true in those areas of our lives where we have regrets. Nothing can change anything we have done in the past. But concentrating on what's happening right now gives us much more control in doing things better. God wants us to focus on the job at hand and move forward in hope.

 NOTES

Storm clouds roll in over Millstreet, Co. Cork

SEPTEMBER 23RD

'A boat, yacht or ship is useless unless it has access to a harbour for shelter.'
~Author Unknown

St. Augustine put it well by saying our hearts are never at rest until they rest in the Lord. It is good to have access to somewhere safe and secure in this world to retreat to. Every single one of us needs some form of shelter from those severe and serious storms of life. We also need shelter from a world whose pace is constant, demanding and often unforgiving.

You Lord, are our shelter and our harbour.
Protect and guide us, when life and all around us gets rough and stormy.
Protect and guide those who are close and near to us.
Amen.

 NOTES:

A Year in Reflection

Magnetism: Drops of rainwater cling onto this yellow flower at Garnish island, West Cork

SEPTEMBER 24TH

God doesn't want our deeds. God wants the love that prompts them.
~Teresa Of Avila

There is an old story told about a king's servant who came upon a spring of delicious water. After filling his leather bag with it, he began the daylong journey to present the water to the king. The king drank with great relish and thanked him profusely. After the servant had left, the King's advisor asked for permission to taste the water. When he did he nearly spat it out because it was warm and stale. "Why did you pretend to enjoy the water?" asked his advisor. The king replied, "It wasn't the water that I was enjoying, it was the love of the servant who brought it to me." Every day people extend gestures of warmness, kindness and love towards me. Sometimes I'm not ready, othertimes I'm not aware of what's been given to me. Today is a day to appreciate all the love shown to me by my family, friends and those closest to me.

 NOTES

The oratory of St. Finbarr, at Gougane Barra, West Cork

SEPTEMBER 25TH

'History is who we are and why we are the way we are.'
~David McCullough

We in Cork have been described as energetic and fun loving by nature. I think few of us can argue with that and we owe much of this to St. Finbarr whose feast day is today and who is the patron saint of Cork. We know that he lived in Gougane Barra as a hermit. Against a backdrop of rugged hills, lake, rivers and streams, Finbarr found great peace. But God gently called Finbarr onto greater things. He moved up the River Lee to find a monastic settlement, from which our present city of Cork grew. Much has been said about Finbarr but he was deeply proud of his faith and what he believed in. It brought him energy and life and he shared it with many. Today is a day of blessing and celebration here in Cork. We ask his blessings on ourselves, our families, our communities, our city and our diocese today. May St. Finbarr continue to guide and direct us each day.

NOTES:

A Year in Reflection

Autumn colours at Myross Wood Retreat House, Leap, West Cork

SEPTEMBER 26TH

'The first person who has to believe in you is you.'
~Author Unknown

It is always important to believe in ourselves and in what we have to offer
and give. Surprisingly many people are slow to believe in themselves. A
child or adult whose gifts and talents are not nurtured will believe over
time that they are simply no good. That is why words of encouragement
are crucial and vital whatever our age. We are often told that God loves
us no matter what. But unless we first believe in ourselves how can we
believe that even God loves us? Whatever your circumstances,
whatever your current situation, you have got to believe in what you can
do. None of us can change the world at large, but my little bit can make
the world of a difference. Our prayer is very short and simple for today,
Lord, help me to believe in myself.

NOTES

Desperation!: A poster advertising ways of raising money for People In Need

SEPTEMBER 27TH

'Even if you are on the right track, you'll get run over if you just sit there.'
~Will Rogers

We can never take anything for granted. What may seem certain and strong isn't always the case. It is easy to sit back and assume that everything will be just fine. It is easy to sit back and drift along in life hoping for the best. We need to be the first to move on from just sitting there and begin to do something. In our Gospels Jesus always knew when it was time to move on to the next village and community.

Every person he met was treated with respect and given time. Nothing was taken for granted. People sometimes say that they are going round in circles or feel boxed in. Every circle can be broken. Every day presents us with an opportunity to do so. But little can happen if we just sit around hoping something might happen.

NOTES:

A Year in Reflection

Curiosity: A young calf checks out roadworks on the Kenmare/Glengarrif Road

SEPTEMBER 28TH

'Memories made from love can never fade'
~Author Unknown

These beautiful words can be our inspiration as well. Every day we generate memories. Sometimes we quickly forget them, sometimes they are best forgotten, but the ones that are built on and around love are the ones that can never fade. What does the word love mean here? It has its roots in God and it has been given to every single person. It is built on trust and acceptance, it is built on openness and honesty and it is built on giving life our best shot. If we can look back on any given day and say that we have memories that were built around love it will have been a good day. In God's eyes it will have been an even better day.

Notes

Ross Castle through the trees at Killarney National Park

SEPTEMBER 29TH

'Know that everything you do comes back to you. Step outside yourself and consider the consequence before you make a move. If your action will bring peace to yourself, it's the right thing to do.'
~Tavis Smiley

The greatest pitfall in the world and in our lives is thinking that our actions do not have an impact on anyone else. Everything we do, good or bad, does make an impact. Isaac Newton's most famous science law states that every action has an equal and opposite reaction. Science also translates into real life. So if we choose something that we know in our hearts is wrong then we can be sure that it is indeed wrong. But if we instead choose something good and positive we can indeed be sure that the benefits will be great. Even if we ignore our inner voice, God never closes the door on anyone. God never wants to knock us, we do enough of it ourselves.

NOTES:

Fruits of autumn in Myross Wood, Leap, West Cork

SEPTEMBER 30TH

*'Know that you are the perfect age. Each year is special and precious,
for you shall only live it once.'*
~Louise Hay

It is fair to say that we sometimes wish we were younger and could turn back the clock. In looking back it is easy to say to ourselves that we could have done so much more and could have done things so different. But, at that particular moment in time, it seemed the right option or we may have had no other choice available. But whatever age we are now is indeed the perfect age. God always encourages us to do what we can, with what we have and to do it to the best of our ability. Wouldn't it be great if we could say that, whatever our age, we're happy with our lot. We ask God's help in making the most of today and everyday right up to our next birthday. It will then be time to look back in thanksgiving and to look forward in hope.

 NOTES

OCTOBER

Stonewashed cottage on the Blasket Island, Co. Kerry

OCTOBER 1ST

'Simplicity is making the journey of this life with just baggage enough.'
~Author Unknown

Today is the feast of St. Therese and she is one of the most popular saints of our time. Her huge appeal is not that she did extra ordinary things but that she did the little things extraordinarily well. She found that she was closest to God when she was doing the simplest and most mundane tasks. The spectacular and sensational always attracts interest and sometimes hype. This was never a part of her life. It is comforting to know that in the simple and ordinary events of our lives that we can be quite close to God. For Therese she dedicated all the seemingly thankless and boring jobs to God. She often said, "I am doing this out of love for you my God." We could do well to reflect on where Therese found happiness and it was always within her reach.

 NOTES:

Patchwork cloud formation over Tooreenbawn, Millstreet, Co. Cork

OCTOBER 2ND

'Angels are direct creations of God, each one a unique Master's piece.'
~Eileen Freeman

Today is the feast of our guardian angel. There are over 300 separate references to angels in the Bible. They are associated with beauty, peace, joy, protection, fulfilment, laughter and love. Every single person has a guardian angel, with no exceptions. Our guardian angel stays with us from birth until our transition back to heaven. They always want to bring us closer to God, they are always journeying with us and gently guiding us through each day. Some may doubt their existence but all the evidence points to these angels as real, active, relevant and the closest friends we can have in this world. We thank God today for this constant loving care. We especially thank these heavenly beings whose joy it is to walk with us through each day.

 NOTES

White fuschia catches the available light in Myross Wood, Leap, West Cork

OCTOBER 3RD

'The principal was visiting first class and asked the students what they wanted to be when they would grow up. A hand shot up. "I want to be possible," the boy answered. "Possible?" the principal asked. "Of all things that you might want to be, why do you want that?" The boy replied, "Because at home my mum and dad are always saying that I'm impossible."

It is easy to label someone as impossible. It is just as easy for them to think that they are indeed impossible, loose self confidence and not believe in themselves. God never sees anyone or any situation as impossible. The constant message throughout scriptures is how God makes the impossible, possible. God always believes in us and always believes that we are indeed full of possibility. Today is a day when I can make something good and positive in my life possible.

NOTES:

'Maxi' a Dalmation savours the moment on Rathcooney hill, Cork

OCTOBER 4TH

'While you are proclaiming peace with your lips, be careful to have it
even more fully in your heart.'
~St. Francis Of Assisi

Today is the feast of St. Francis and he is one of those rare saints who has managed to capture the attention and admiration of the entire world. His life has inspired people of all ages and the appeal of this saint, cuts across national boundaries and religious differences.

He is most famous for his respect towards God, his simple life and his tender love and attention to all creation. Many animals and especially pets will get a special treat today in honour of St. Francis. The life of Francis still challenges all of us today. The invitation is to sort through our lives and discard the unnecessary and useless. Don't we all need to do it. Today could be the day to start.

NOTES

Speed: A motocross biker in full flight at Vernon Mount, Cork

OCTOBER 5TH

'I believe that God loves each one of us without condition, no matter what we ever do or say or think or feel.'
~Nina Herrmann

A farmer placed a weathercock inscribed with the sentence, "God is love" on the top of his barn. One day a traveller noticing the weathercock, stopped to look and with a smirk on his face asked the farmer: "Do you think that God's love can change so lightly like the wind vane you've got up there?" The farmer shook his head and replied: "No my friend. That is meant to show that whichever way the wind blows, 'God is love'." For all of us life is constantly changing and turning. In the middle of all of life's changes and in the middle of all of life's ups and downs, God's love for us is always constant. We are free to accept that love, reject it or go it alone. But for those who choose to accept that love, the benefits are great.

 NOTES:

Cian Murphy is all smiles with his goat for Bothar at Rathcooney, Cork

OCTOBER 6TH

'We dream of doing great things when all the time we are called to brighten one little spot.'
~Author Unknown

What a beautiful piece of wisdom and something we could keep close to us each day. We have great plans, great ideas and great hopes. It's good to have all of these but there is never a guarantee that any of them will happen. God is gently calling us to do much less. We are called to brighten one spot and that spot is where we are right now. We are called to do our bit, to do our best and after that we can do no more. To brighten our little spot or to brighten that of someone else, is infinitely better than trying to piece together many great things.

 NOTES

Apple Delight: Organic apples ready for picking at Myross Wood Retreat House, Leap, West Cork

OCTOBER 7TH

'Anyone can count the seeds in an apple, but only God can count the
number of apples in a seed.'
~Robert Schuller

Sometimes we think we know all the answers, that we know our boundaries, that we know a lot of things about ourselves and other people. But we don't have the overall view like God does. No one can ever get this overall view, it is beyond our limitations. No fortune teller or crystal ball can predict the overall view. Some people become obsessed in trying to find out what tomorrow or next year might bring. A lot of wasted energy goes into predicting stuff that's outside our control. But we can put our trust in God, who has a much better sense of the overall plan. We begin by putting our trust in God to get us through this day.

NOTES:

OCTOBER 7TH

A Year in Reflection

'Stairway To Heaven' at Garnish Island, West Cork

OCTOBER 8TH

'Limitations live only in our minds. But if we use our imaginations,
our possibilities become endless.'
~J Paolinetti

If we could see every limitation before us then we would get little done during any day. It is true that we are limited in what we can do and that we can't do everything no matter how much we think we can. It is also true that many limitations live only in our minds. What we think of as a limitation may in fact be a stepping stone to something much better and more positive in our lives. God always provides stepping stones for us. These can help us move forward with our lives and help our possibilities become possible.

 NOTES

Smile!: A farmer had a great sense of humour with these round bales near Bantry, West Cork

OCTOBER 9TH

'Let no one ever come to you without leaving better and happier. Be the living expression of God's kindness: kindness in your face, kindness in your eyes and kindness in your smile.'
~Mother Teresa

We totally underestimate what we can bring to other people. Our physical presence sends out signals that are easily picked up by others. Our body language can often say much about ourselves even before we speak a word. It goes without saying that if our outer expression is a positive one, then that will also rub off and touch other people. It is much easier to smile at someone rather than have a long face. Of course people have genuine reasons to be feeling under the weather all of which need to be respected. But for the most part we could certainly radiate a little more kindness in our outer expression and a smile will always go a long way.

 NOTES:

Time Zone: Clocks showing the different times around the world in New York, U.S.

OCTOBER 10TH

Time is too slow for those who wait, too swift for those who fear, too long for those who grieve and too short for those who rejoice but for those who love, time is eternal.
~Author Unknown

How often we have said that time goes so quickly. There is much to do, see, accomplish and achieve and never enough time to do it all. But with God time is eternal. This can only mean that God doesn't have shares in Rolex or Quartz! We may never have enough time for all we want to do but with God there is plenty time for everything. When we make time to love and nurture love we are in a timeless place. It is also a place where we are indeed very close to God.

 NOTES

Walkway through the woods at Myross Wood, Leap, West Cork

OCTOBER 11TH

'Two roads diverged in a wood and I took the one less travelled by.
And that made all the difference.'
~Robert Frost (Poet)

Life as we know goes at a hectic pace. Life is made up of many journeys but it seems that many of our journeys are spent travelling with pressures, deadlines, stress and making up for lost time. Journeys or roads less travelled are the ones that make time for ourselves. These roads are quietness, relaxation, a walk on a summer's evening, silence, gentle music and just time out in general. Such journeys or roads are special and can make all the difference. They are not difficult to find and in fact are quite plentiful around us. What makes them unique is that so few use them. God encourages us to use them as often as we can and to feel the difference.

NOTES:

A Year in Reflection

Bravery: A surfer turns in on a wave off the coast of California, U.S.

OCTOBER 12TH

'Don't run through life so fast that you forget not only where you've been but also where you're going. Life is not a race but a journey to be savoured every step of the way.'
~Author Unknown

It seems silly to say that we could forget where we've been and where we're going. But on closer reflection we are in fact racing through life and we are packing so much into our days that we can indeed loose track. If our journey through life is to be savoured, we certainly need to slow down or at least make a good attempt at doing so. No one is going to make that space for us. We have to make it. You are surely worth it. Such space gives us the chance to wind down and enjoy all the blessings that God has given us. If we can't enjoy these then we really have missed the whole point of living. The pace of life may be fast but importantly we have control over the pace of our lives.

 NOTES

Hard Work: A Jack Russell has just about enough time for a yawn with her litter of beautiful pups.

OCTOBER 13TH

'99% of failures come from people who have a habit of making excuses.'
~George Washington

A fisherman went fishing and caught a big fish. But as he removed it from the hook it slipped from his hand to disappear back into the sea. Annoyed to have let such a good fish go, he cast his line out again. This time he caught a much smaller fish, he unhooked it very cautiously and carefully put it back into his container. At that moment an onlooker approached the fisherman and asked him, "Why did you throw the big one back into the water and only keep the small one?" The fisherman was quick to reply, "Oh my frying pan is small and wouldn't be able to hold that big fish!" We may not always come up with such a quick answer but too many excuses do eventually catch up with us. Can I be big enough to say that I have made a mistake or will I resort to excuses?

 NOTES:

A Year in Reflection

Autumn Colours: The sun really captures the beauty of this autumnal scene at Fota gardens, near Cobh, Co. Cork

OCTOBER 14TH

'As long as you can still be disappointed, you're still young.'
~Joyce Cary

Disappointments are part and parcel of life. Some we expect, some just happen and more happen totally unexpected. While they do set us back, we can certainly pick up the pieces and get going again. In most cases we re-adjust, we learn from the experience and move on. Trying to avoid disappointments is impossible; it's restrictive and means we are out of touch with real life. Even in our Gospels, Jesus and his friends experienced setbacks and disappointments. Everything did not go according to plan, not everyone welcomed them but yet they kept going forward in hope. An old saying probably sums it up best, 'Our best success comes after our greatest disappointments.'

 NOTES

A Year in Reflection

St. Declan's round tower at Ardmore, Co. Waterford

OCTOBER 15TH

'All prayers are answered if we are willing to admit that sometimes the answer is no.'
Àuthor Unknown

A five year old child walked into the kitchen to find his mum baking scones. He stood watching her. After a while, he asked, "Can I have one, please?" " Not before your tea" his mother replied. The child ran to his bedroom in tears. Very soon he returned with the message, "God said it's ok to have a scone now." "But God didn't tell me that" his mother replied. To which the child was quick to reply, "You mustn't have been listening!"

It's good to know that every prayer is answered even if the answer is sometimes yes and sometimes no. One can never waste time in praying. We can waste time in various ways but time spent in prayer is always quality time. Quality thrives in small short bursts and especially when applied to prayer.

NOTES:

A Year in Reflection

A shower of rain transforms the beauty of these leaves at Tooreenbawn, Millstreet

OCTOBER 16TH

'A year from now you may wish you had started today.'
~Karen Lamb

We may have some plans for next weekend but that is still a few days off yet. We may have some idea of what we might be doing in a month's time but little idea of our circumstances in a year's time.

We often keep looking ahead in life but never look at where we are right now. The gospel message constantly focuses in on what is happening today. In fact the language used is quite strong. Someone who plans for the future without an eye on today is called a fool. Today will always shape the future. A good decision or choice made today could be the best investment we will ever make. Not to do so could mean disappointments and frustration further down the road.

 NOTES

A wave crashes into rocks near Ballyferriter, Co. Kerry

OCTOBER 17TH

'All rivers run to the sea yet the sea is not full.
~Ecclesiastes 1:7

This is a beautiful image reminding us that we have so much to give no matter what our age. It is good to be open to learning and to be open to something fresh and different in life. We have given so much already, we are doing our best to lead by good example and learn from our own experiences. Yet we also have so much more to give. No one person can say that they have it all worked out or that they can give no more. Our contribution to this world is crucially important. In God's eyes your contribution is the most special of all. That is why the sea is never full. God loves your contribution. Whether it's a drop or a flood every contribution is valuable. Today I can begin to believe in myself and that what I am giving is appreciated, valued and cherished, especially by God.

NOTES:

'Transformation' The arrival of autumn brings a multitude of colour among the blackberry leaves at Ballyvolane, Cork

OCTOBER 18TH

'The value of compassion cannot be over-emphasized. Anyone can criticize. It takes a true believer to be compassionate. The greatest burdens are lifted when one feels cared for and understood.
~Arthur Stainback.

We live in a world that can sometimes be cold, cruel and impersonal. Every community does its best to counter these but it's not an easy task. Today is the feast of St. Luke. He wrote one of the Gospels and presents Jesus as someone who had a tender compassion for everyone. In the gospel of Luke, every person no matter how sad or ugly their story, were always within the reach of the Lord's compassion. Luke was a doctor himself who always had hope and wrote with great optimism and joy. Today's feast day encourages us to be compassionate in all we do or say. Luke is the patron saint of doctors and surgeons. Today we ask the Lord to bless their great work.

NOTES

Friendly yawn at Fota Wildlife Park

OCTOBER 19TH

'One of the main reasons why people are not doing well is because they keep trying to get through the day. A more worthy challenge is what I can get from this day.'
~Jim Rohn

Today may be one of those days that didn't get off to the best of starts. We may have been sluggish with our energy levels slow to kick in. When we are simply trying to get through the day it usually drags. It becomes routine, monotonous and boring. But every day has the potential to be a good day, a day when I can learn something new or do something I didn't do yesterday. Every day will be a mixture from the great to the awful and from what's ordinary to what's enjoyable. Every day will be a challenge. But an even bigger challenge is how today can be different because of what I am giving to it and how I am open to learning from it.

 NOTES:

A Year in Reflection

'Fast v Slow' at Robert's Cove, near Carrigaline, Co. Cork

OCTOBER 20TH

Try reading this!

Timeisthecoinofyourlifeitistheonlycoinyouhaveandonlyyoucandeterminehowitwillbespent
becarefulbecauseotherpeoplewillspenditforyou

Trying to read that would give you a headache! But that is the way life is for many people. It is at a hectic pace, all rushed and packed into each other. The above line is harder to read without breaks and full stops. Our lives are on the same level too because there isn't enough time to pause, slow down and reflect. There isn't enough time to focus in on the really important things in life. When such time isn't given something else gives. Right throughout the gospels we have accounts of Jesus taking time out just to be with his friends or by himself. Life may be a jumble because of its pace. I can choose to be a part of the jumble or I can choose to be much more in control.

 NOTES

'Orange Sunrise' over Blandford, Dorset, England

OCTOBER 21ST

'When nothing seems to help, I go and look at a stonecutter hammering away at his rock perhaps a hundred times without as much as a crack showing. Yet at the hundred and first blow it will split in two and I know it was not that blow that did it, but all that had gone before.'
~Jacob Riis

During this month of October and usually around now we focus in on missionary work across the world. Many people that we know and love here in Cork have dedicated some or all of their lives to working with the poorest of the poor. Some may say that such missionary work is a waste of time and is like throwing a tiny drop of water into the ocean. But like the stonecutter hammering away, the great work of these men and women, has made a huge difference and will continue to do so. We pray for all missionaries and the people they work with across the world.

 NOTES:

OCTOBER 21ST

Harbour views at Portmagee, Co. Kerry

OCTOBER 22ND

'Nothing would be done at all if we waited until we could do it
so well, that no one could find fault with it.'
~John Henry Newman

It is part and parcel of everyone to have some fault. No one is perfect, and we all have some weak point. What we do each day will always have some fault or weak point. But why put the spotlight on what is weak, when there is so much more that has been done well by us?
Why worry about what others might think even if we have done our best?
We can't please everyone and God is always pleased with us when we can say, "I have done my best", "I have done my bit"
"I enjoyed doing that" "I have no complaints". In God's eyes our faults and weaker points can be stepping stones rather than stumbling blocks.

 NOTES

'Delivery Time!' Mandy arrives with all of Cork's latest news

OCTOBER 23RD

'If opportunity doesn't knock, build a door.'
~Milton Berle

Wouldn't it be great if everything just happened the way we want. It rarely does and we must often take the first step to make it happen. Too many just sit back and wait for something to happen. There are no magic wands in this world but there is plenty of possibility and will power within each of us to make things happen. In the advertising world it's all about getting noticed. It's about the right colours, the right words and the right catchphrase. It's up to us too to get noticed. We have such a reserve of potential. The gospel message is to share this reserve, to let our light shine and to get noticed and be noticed.

Every little chink of light no matter how small is always noticed.

 NOTES:

Orange Carpet: Only the season of autumn could come up with such beauty at Fota Gardens, near Cobh

OCTOBER 24TH

'You're not wealthy until you have something money can't buy'
~Author Unknown

We never had it easier with banking and getting access to our accounts and money. Cheque books, laser and credit cards, e-banking and credit unions have make it all so easy. Many judge wealth by what they own, by what they have materially and by the size of our bank account. But from God's point of view we're not really wealthy until we have something money can't buy. This could be many things, real friends, health, peace of mind, happy in what we're doing, healing, love, an ability to forgive and so much more. Money can buy a lot of things but it certainly cannot buy everything. When we have what it can't buy then we are indeed truly wealthy.

 NOTES

A Year in Reflection

'Wind Power' A yacht making great progress out of Dingle Bay, Co.Kerry

OCTOBER 25TH

'I can't change the direction of the wind but I can adjust
my sails to always reach my destination.'
~J Dean

There are many things in life that are outside our control. Sometimes this causes a lot of stress and worry. But what's outside our control should never stop us on our own journey. I can adjust and adapt even when life is not going well for me. God always wants to help us in reaching our destination. Today we ask God to help all of us on our daily journey and in particular those days when it seems we are being blown off course.

NOTES:

Morning Fog: These cattle are waking up to a mixture of October sunshine and fog near Castlemartyr, Co. Cork

OCTOBER 26TH

"The apostles said to the Lord, "Increase our faith." The Lord replied, "Were your faith the size of a mustard seed you could say to this mulberry tree: Be uprooted and planted in the sea and it would obey you."

~Luke 17:5-6

Only faith can answer the most profound questions of life. It gives hope and meaning to life. Just because we believe doesn't mean we have all the answers. Faith is all about trust and at the end of the day it is all about a relationship with God. One never looses ones faith but one can stop shaping our lives by it. It also happens to be the greatest power and energy in the world and that's why Jesus compared it to a mustard seed. It is so small that you could hardly hold it in your fingers and no bigger than the size of the full stop at the end of this sentence. Yet it grows into a fine big tree. With faith what looks impossible becomes possible.

 NOTES

A Year in Reflection

'Give Us This Day Our Daily Bread' An interpretation of the Lord's prayer at the Monkstown Flower Festival

OCTOBER 27TH

'Sometimes our light goes out but is blown into flame by another human being. Each of us owes deepest thanks to those who have rekindled this light.'
~ Albert Schweitzer

We can all recall times in our lives when we were in trouble, when our options were limited, when it seemed our light had gone out. But some person in our lives made all the difference and got us back on track again. It may have been a parent, brother, sister, grandparent, partner, friend or may even have been the inspiration of an outsider. We owe this person our deepest thanks. Today we can say a quiet little prayer for them. As we say think of them, we know that we can also now blow into flame the darkened light of somebody else. The fact that we have been there before should be enough inspiration.

NOTES:

A Year in Reflection

A sample of some of the beautiful art work on display in the Scoil Oilibheir Art Day, Ballyvolane, Cork

OCTOBER 28TH

'Life is a great big canvas, throw all the paint you can on it.'
~Danny Kaye

If only we could see each day as a new beginning and a fresh start. We keep bringing so much from yesterday with us. Like a canvas we may have used the wrong colours yesterday. Who hasn't? We all look back and say 'If only I didn't do that.' But we can do so much more today. We can choose our own colours, we can choose to make this day as good as we can. If we use the image of colour, then God sends us many and varied colours. We are never stuck to one colour. Life should never be a mixture of boredom, staleness and drabness. God's invitation is to move from this to something else. Life and especially today is given to us to make the most of it. We're not all Michelangelo but we're good enough to make a real go of what God has given to us.

NOTES

Letting Go: Even as we head for the month of October there is so much autumn colour to be found out and about including Kilbarry, Cork

OCTOBER 29TH

'A diamond is a chunk of coal that has been made good under pressure.'
~Author Unknown

It seems most unlikely that a dirty chunk of coal could have such potential to become something beautiful and precious. It might seem that there are parts of our lives as well with little potential. But it is these parts that are worth giving every chance to grow. No one likes to be under pressure, but difficulties and challenges always push us onto another level. Right throughout the Gospels we have examples of people who experienced major knocks in life but experienced a great sense of peace when they met Jesus. A lump of coal is lifeless and a diamond sparkles with life. Today we ask God to breathe new life into what is lifeless and stale in our lives. What is old, stale and most unlikely can undergo radical change for our own good.

 NOTES:

Bathtime: Any day is good for a bath especially at Ballylickey, West Cork

OCTOBER 30TH

'Find the courage to ask for what you want. Others have the right to tell you yes or no, but you always have the right to ask. Likewise, everybody has the right to ask you for what they want and you have the right to say no or yes.

~Don Ruiz

The key question here is what do I want? What do I want or need right now that will bring some benefit to my life? There is a big difference between someone who is over demanding and selfish and the one who asks for what is good and important. Equally we can also ask God for what we want. Every prayer, petition or request will always be answered. Sometimes it's not in the way we expected or in the way we wanted but God also has that right too to say yes or no.

NOTES

Imelda Burke and Katrinia Kelleher getting into the spirit of Halloween!

OCTOBER 31ST

'It is said that sheep may get lost simply by nibbling away at grass and never looking up. That can also be true for any of us. We can focus so much on what is immediately before us that we fail to see life in larger perspective.'
~Donald Bitsberger

As we are about to move from this month of October into November there is a sense of time slipping by very quickly. There's a bit of the sheep in all of us. We're so busy doing what's near at hand that we often let the essentials slip through us. Not even a spooky Halloween can get us to look up. There are many reasons to look up. Looking up gives us the chance to see what's happening in our lives. All that's going well will give us renewed confidence to keep going. Whatever needs to be improved can also be done. This changeover of months is always a good time to lift our heads for a quick review.

 NOTES:

NOVEMBER

A tree holding on to its last few leaves as we enter the month of November at Fota Gardens, near Cobh, Co. Cork

November 1st

'A person does not have to be an angel to be a saint.'
~Albert Schweitzer

There was an elderly couple living at a corner near a school. The children had a habit of cutting across their lawn and of course wore an ugly path through it, especially when it rained. At first it annoyed the couple and then it angered them. As the weeks went on, they realised this problem was destroying their peace of mind. They prayed about it, talked about it and then one day came up with a solution. They put gravel through the path and lined the sides with flowers. The response was amazing. The children thanked the couple for the path and even asked the names of the flowers. In short this couple had become living Saints. Today's feast of All Saints, is not just about a select few but is a celebration of lots of people who did things very well over time.

 Notes:

Kilcatherine cemetery, between Allihies and Eyeries, West Cork

NOVEMBER 2ND

'If the people we love are taken from us, the way to have them live on is to never stop loving them. Buildings burn, people die but real love is forever.'
~Author Unknown

Irish people have a great respect for the dead. During this month of November many will visit a cemetery, say a prayer for a loved one who has died and decorate a grave with a flower or a nightlight. Whether or not one should pray for the dead is one of the great arguments that divide Christians. Any prayer is always good. Praying for those who have died is also a good thing. In prayer we stand in God's presence and in praying for those who have died we are in some way connected with them. Today, the feast of 'All Souls', is a day to pray for those who have died. Our nearest and dearest who have gone on before us will always have a special place in our hearts. They will never be forgotten.

 NOTES

'Hope in Darkness' as the sun breaks through the darkest of clouds on the road between Youghal and Midleton, Co. Cork

NOVEMBER 3RD

'Do more than exist, live. Do more than touch, feel. Do more than look, observe. Do more than read, absorb. Do more than hear, listen. Do more than think, ponder. Do more than talk, do something.'
~John Roads.

All of us are called to do that little bit more. It is being alert to those little things that could pass us by. November may be a month when life and light seem to be scarce. For many it is a month simply to get through. We can get through any month and any day when we are alive to what God has given to us. God is our guiding light, our hope for today, our inspiration to keep going, our energy to do that little bit more. It is also worth keeping an eye out for those who will need that little bit more love, support and encouragement during this month of November.

 NOTES:

Rough Atlantic waves crash on the Kerry coastline near Ballyferriter

NOVEMBER 4TH

'If you treat someone as they are, they will remain as they are. If you treat them as they ought to be and could be, they will become what they ought to be and could be.'
~Goethe

We all like to be treated well and fairly. It is a natural human instinct. Even Jesus in our gospels spoke of it many times by asking us to treat others as we would like them to treat us. Every single one of us has the potential to go that extra step. We have the potential to give, use and develop all that God has given to us that little bit more. Other people also have that same potential. But we sometimes treat others as if they are incapable of change. What a shame if that were to happen. We are encouraged to nurture the potential, the promise, the goodness and all the great things within each person with no exceptions.

 NOTES

Flood waters next to the Lee Road, Cork

NOVEMBER 5TH

'Love is the river of life in the world.'
~Henry Beecher

Streams and rivers run through every valley and plain. They all have one destination and that is the ocean. The one thing they all have in common is the river bank on both sides. This is crucial to the life of the river. If it's not there the river flows out to become a lake or a floodplain. It loses its life and energy. In short it's going nowhere.

The image of a riverbank is one that can best describe God's presence in our lives. Like the river bank God gently guides us along, on our own daily journeys. We need support, direction and gentle guidance on our own journey. The bank of a river may seem insignificant or not very important. Remove that bank and the river is helpless. Remove God from our lives and we are also indeed helpless.

 NOTES:

Beautiful dentures at Millstreet Green Glens Equestrian Centre!

NOVEMBER 6TH

'The best way to realize how much faith you have is to offer
to help someone find or renew theirs.'
~Author Unknown

It is never possible to measure faith like we do when we measure height or weight. Our belief in a God who loves us is the main cornerstone of our faith. Everything else is built from and around this cornerstone. Some people may be struggling to find or even see this cornerstone. We can gently point the way forward by doing our best with what we have and leading by good example. When this is done quietly and without fuss the results can often be extraordinary. Helping someone to find or renew their faith may not always be our first priority. But we often do it without even realizing it.

 NOTES

Twisty road up through the Healy Pass, West Cork

NOVEMBER 7TH

'You'll learn more about a road by travelling it than by consulting all the maps in the world.'
~Author Unknown

Maps have been around for hundreds of years since the first explorers started discovering different parts of our world. Today maps have been replaced more by satellite navigation systems. We're told they're more reliable and accurate in getting us to our destination. But modern technology and different maps can never tell us the feel of a road and its character. The only way to find out is by travelling along it. The same goes in life. All our journeys are uniquely different. All roads in life have their many twists and turns. Some uphill, some down, but all going in the one direction. God is our map and compass, guiding us through all of life's journeys.

 NOTES:

Tranquil Barley Lake, near Glengarriff, West Cork

NOVEMBER 8TH

'Giving is better than receiving because giving starts the receiving process.'
~Jim Rohn

There is a story told about a miser who fell into a well. Even though he wasn't liked in the village because of his meanness, the people were anxious to rescue the man. Someone stretched down and said "Give me your hand." The miser hadn't given anything in his life and could not understand what giving his hand meant. Someone else shouted down the well "Take my hand." Instantly the miser stretched out his hand and was pulled from the well. Giving and receiving always go hand in hand. We receive a lot when we are allowed to give. One of the greatest enemies of God is a meanness of spirit. We are called to be generous with our time, our love, our energy, our gifts and talents. Is there a bit of a miser in me, in how I use what God has given to me?

 NOTES

A Year in Reflection

November sunset over the Atlantic Ocean, Castlegregory, Co. Kerry

NOVEMBER 9TH

'Maybe if we were charged a fee to pray we would have a better sense of its value. Of course no one could afford it, for the value of prayer is priceless.'
~Vickie Girard

Today we hear a lot about things that are important and good for us. The difficulty of course is trying to squeeze all these into our busy lives. Prayer is probably the best example. Like a wheel in motion we have too much momentum to slow down and pause for prayer. If you find it hard to slow down, remember that it is only hard to you because in itself it is easy. Prayer is all about taking time out for ourselves. It is a willingness to speak to God through words, through silence, through music and so on. Short bursts of prayer are the best of all. Thankfully prayer is one of the best free gifts going and no booming economy can match its priceless value.

 NOTES:

View through the trees at Conna Castle, Co. Cork

NOVEMBER 10TH

'There's no way to make people like change. You can only make
them feel less threatened by it.'
~Frederick Hayes

Change is part and parcel of life. Significant changes are part of our lives too. Some are forced, some are necessary and some are welcome. By and large any change needs adjustments on our behalf. During this month of November we remember and pray for those who have died. For those who have lost a loved one, the changes can be overwhelming and traumatic. Adjusting to the change of a loved one not around any more can be a slow, painful and lonely journey. Our prayers during this month of November are not just a token gesture of doing something for the sake of doing it. Our prayers are in some small way an attempt to help us cope with these changes. We may never get over some changes in life but we can go a long way in feeling less threatened by them.

 NOTES

Boat at rest at Lamb's Head, Co. Kerry

November 11th

When he had finished speaking he said to Simon, "put out into deep water and pay out your nets for a catch." "Master" Simon replied, "we worked hard all night long and caught nothing but if you say so I will pay out the nets." And when they had done this they netted such a huge number of fish that their nets began to tear.
~Luke 5:4-7

There is a lovely message to this story. We can all relate to times when we feel let down by God, when we have tried everything and caught nothing. It is so easy to throw in the towel. Yet the call is to put our trust in God. God never abandons us or never tries to outsmart us. Once we are willing to take that initiative and put our trust in God, then we are ready to face anything life may throw at us.

 Notes:

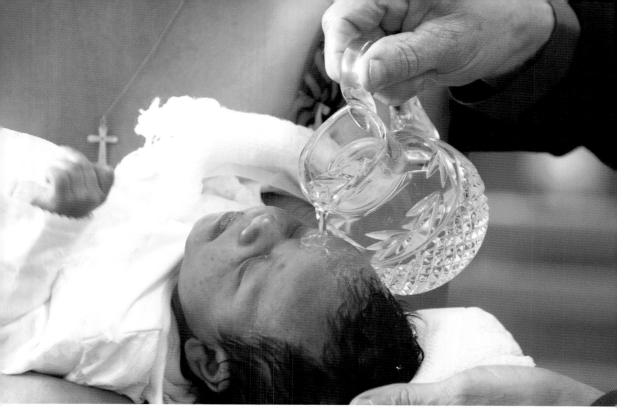

Baby Rebecca Folarumni Akinkuolie is baptised in St. Oliver's Church, Ballyvolane, Cork

NOVEMBER 12TH

'A great deal of what we see depends on what we're looking for.'
~Author Unknown

If we all experienced the same thing each day, our lives would be very boring. Everyone's experience is just so different each day and of course it all depends on what we're looking for. If our expectations are high and unrealistic the chances are we're going to be disappointed.

If our demands of other people are too high then we are sure to be disappointed. In our gospels Jesus says to look for small things first. He spoke about a tiny little mustard seed growing into the biggest tree of them all. When we're looking for little and small we will find plenty. They all do add up to something substantial. Today I can look for something good in my life. It may be small, it may seem insignificant but within the bigger picture it is the most precious of all.

 NOTES

A Year in Reflection

Ruins of an old cottage on the Blasket Island, Co. Kerry

NOVEMBER 13TH

'There is nothing more dreadful than the habit of doubt. Doubt separates people. It is a poison that disintegrates friendships and breaks up pleasant relationships. It is a thorn that constantly irritates and hurts.'
~G. Siddharta

To doubt is a normal human reaction. But to linger in doubt and constantly question or disbelieve can create lots of problems. Excessive doubts stifle healthy growth. In our Gospels Jesus constantly eroded doubts in people's minds. He instilled in them a self belief and a confidence in their own unique ability and worth. The same goes for us too. We may doubt our own abilities and those around us. We need to be convinced that we can deliver. We can be forever waiting for others to make it happen but it's only we ourselves who can really make it happen.

 NOTES:

Bare branches reaching for the sky at Fota Gardens, Co. Cork

NOVEMBER 14TH

'One of the deepest impulses is the impulse to record, to scratch a drawing on something, to etch a name on a tree, to rub a stone off a wall or to keep a diary. This instinct of recording the present into the past is the very basis of civilisation.'
~John Chapman

All of us are shaped today by all that has happened in the past. We need to realize that the life, culture and experience of those gone before us still have an influence in our lives. That is why during this month of November we pray for those who have died in a special way. Some might ask why March or April wasn't picked when new life is in abundance all around in nature. But November has been picked so that we are indeed in touch with the darkness of our own lives and our own significant losses. In remembering all those who have died we acknowledge their influence in our own lives today.

◗ NOTES

Mairead O'Brien relaxing at Nash 19, Princes Street, Cork

NOVEMBER 15TH

'You give but little when you give of your possessions,
it is when you give of yourself that you truly give.'
~Author Unknown

As we journey through November many of us are already thinking of Christmas, gifts and presents. Some call it getting organised ahead of the rush, others call it madness. But at the end of the day it's nice to give and nice to receive. Can one measure giving in terms of possessions? Not really. It fades into insignificance when it's put next to giving in terms of what we can give personally. When we begin to give of our time, our love, our experience, our encouragement, our care, our support, we are truly giving. Perhaps we totally underestimate what we can give to someone and how one small act of kindness can make the world of a difference to someone else.

 NOTES:

A Year in Reflection

Awesome power of the sea at Clogher beach, near Ballyferriter, Co. Kerry

NOVEMBER 16TH

'In the confrontation between the sea and the rock, the sea always wins.
Not just by strength but also through perseverance.'
~Author Unknown

Every time the sea hits an obstacle it will always find a way around it.
It's a good image for us too. When we hit an obstacle or difficulty we
can be sure that there are always ways around it. Sometimes it seems
that no solution can ever be found. With perseverance there is always a
way. From a faith perspective the ability to persevere is all the stronger.
There are so many people who dig deep despite huge obstacles. They
are an inspiration to many more who struggle.

We pray today for the strength to keep going and for that great self
belief - that we can do it no matter what.

NOTES

Winter skyline on the Ring Of Kerry

NOVEMBER 17TH

'If you can find a path with no obstacles it probably doesn't lead anywhere.'
~Frank Clark

We all experience obstacles on our daily journey, some are small and more are much more significant. A clear Gospel message is an acknowledgement of enough obstacles out there without us having to add more. But it seems we like adding what's unnecessary and difficult. We lay obstacles when we carelessly criticise, when we give out about nothing, when we target our anger on others, when we fail to encourage and when we put someone's confidence down. Jesus says, 'why add more unnecessary burdens when there are enough of them out there already?' Maths may be difficult at times but here the equation is simple: Do I add to what's already overloaded? Or can I subtract and take away what's unnecessary and burdensome?

NOTES:

I Love You: Saoirse, the two month old giraffe gets a loving kiss from her mum, Sonya at Fota Wildlife Park, near Cobh, Co. Cork

NOVEMBER 18TH

'They have lost the run of themselves.'
~Old Saying

Many of our old sayings are very interesting and always have some meaning. Behind the above saying is the idea that someone has forgotten their basic essentials. They have forgotten their values, their background and have forgotten their real selves. We might know of someone to whom this applies but on occasions we too forget the run of ourselves. We simply forget the really important and essential things in life. All of us are pilgrims on a journey. We sometimes forget that we are only passing through this world, that we are fragile and limited. We are not invincible. God wants us to do one thing each day and that is simply to learn to be ourselves. It's a great way of connecting with God and every time we do it, we most certainly have not forgotten the run of ourselves.

 NOTES

Jagged rocks near Clogher beach, Co. Kerry

NOVEMBER 19TH

'A person with one watch knows what time it is. A person with two watches is never quite sure.'
~Lee Segal

When the Lotto rolls into huge money everyone plays the game and feels confident of winning. The odds of winning remain very remote even with a big jackpot. But large sums of money don't always buy everything. No sum of money can buy health, peace of mind, real friends, happiness, love and trust. The gospel message always evolves around balance. It's good to have enough to buy the essentials and live comfortably. But no money or plastic card can buy what satisfies our innermost longings. That's the place where God wants to bring a multitude of blessings. Money can't buy them but I'm really rich if I'm at least open to some of these blessings.

🖊 NOTES:

First snow of winter on Caherbarnagh mountain, Co. Cork

NOVEMBER 20TH

'90% of friction in daily life is caused by our tone of voice'

Who would have thought that our voice is so important? We give many clues away as to how we're feeling, through body language. If someone has their arms folded and legs crossed, the chances are high that they're not really interested in what's happening around them. How we speak to others can leave such an impression and make such an impact. Our tone of voice can range from anger, sarcasm, venom, dominance, power, blame, hurt and that's only for starters. It's how others pick up on our tone of voice and it seems the immediate response is negativity and friction. Perhaps today we could keep in mind our words and the way we say them. Our tone of voice could be more gentle and kind, more encouraging and appreciative, more inclusive and welcoming. Less friction means less stress and far more progress each day.

 NOTES

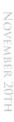

Heading home on a winter's evening at Castletownshend, West Cork

NOVEMBER 21ST

To journey is to go somewhere in particular, to wander is to go nowhere at all. To journey requires direction and purpose, to wander may be to drift or lose the way.'
~Michael Shortall

We all wander in life. We sometimes drift and lose direction on our daily journey. This is not earth shattering or the end of the world. Because we're human it happens to everyone with no exceptions. It is particularly sad though when someone drifts aimlessly in life with no anchor or direction. The best of efforts to stop the drift can often go in vain. When all else seems to fail, our belief in a loving God is a mighty anchor. We may wander and lose direction in life but God is always pulling us gently back and pointing us in the right direction.

 NOTES:

Colourful guitars at the Pro Musica shop on Oliver Plunkett Street, Cork

NOVEMBER 22ND

'There is nothing in the world so much like prayer as music is.'
~William Merrill

Where would we be without music? It expresses feelings and thought and it is above and beyond all words. Everyone's taste in music is different and varied. Most importantly of all it is a gift from God to be enjoyed and savoured. Today is the feast of St. Cecilia, who is the patroness of musicians.

What is your favourite type of music?
Do you use music to relax and unwind or is it something uplifting for you?

Perhaps it's a bit of both. But today is a day to thank God and Cecilia for music in our lives. As the old saying puts it well: 'When words fail, music speaks.'

 NOTES

Fungi growing on a fallen tree at Clondrohid, Co. Cork

November 23rd

'People will try and tell you that all the great opportunities have been snapped up. In reality the world changes every second, blowing new opportunities in all directions, including yours.'
~Ken Hakuta

We're very much aware how our world is constantly changing as we speak. This is not just confined to the weather changing but includes everyone's plans, activities and events for each day. All of these working together generate great energy and generate many possibilities. Some call this chaos, disarray and confusion. With so much to choose from, the worry is that in the end little is chosen. But in our gospels Jesus widened people's choice, widened their horizons and encouraged people to choose the essentials. We too can choose wisely from many opportunities each day.

 Notes:

Evening Prayer: A lovely November skyline silhouettes Blarney Church, near Cork

NOVEMBER 24TH

'Do not worry if you have built your castles in the air. They are where they should be.
Now put the foundations under them.
*~**Henry David Thoreau***

We all know the importance of a strong foundation. It doesn't just apply to buildings but also with relationships, family, friends, work, health, prayer and so on. A foundation that gives way is called subsidence.

We can work on the foundations of different things in our lives long before subsidence begins. At the heart of all scripture readings is that God is the foundation of our own lives and all we do. When we begin to let this go, real subsidence begins.

NOTES

Pathway through Central Park, New York, U.S.

NOVEMBER 25TH

'If we take care of the moments, the years will take care of themselves.'
~Maria Edgeworth

Someone was watching a clockmaker hook a pendulum onto a grandfather clock. The thought came to this person on all the hard work that the clock would have to do. 60 ticks a minute, 3,600 ticks an hour, 86,400 ticks a day, and 604,800 ticks a week. The person asked the clockmaker if the clock would be able for it. He answered, "of course it will. It only has to make one tick at a time." As we head towards the end of November we are moving into a busy time of year. There will be lots happening with much to do. For some it's stressful and difficult.

But we're much more in control when we're doing what we want to do and not what others think we should be doing. One step or one tick at a time is a great reminder of how to get through any day.

NOTES:

Waves crash onto the rocks at Crookhaven, Co. Cork

NOVEMBER 26TH

'Good old days start with good new days, like today.'
~Denise Settle

How often we hear, "in the good old days...." We hear of a simpler lifestyle, plain food and great neighbours. We hear about less money, more hardships but a greater satisfaction with life. We hear of more quality time and a better way of life. Some if not all of these have been slowly eroded with time, affluence and materialism. We certainly need more of the spirit of the good old days. But it's easy just to confine them to the history books and nostalgic talk. The past can never become the present but the spirit of the good old days begins with a good new day like today. It begins with the realisation that it's we ourselves who are always in control of quality time, whether it is with ourselves, family or friends. The good old days begin to blossom when we use quality time to treasure the essentials of life.

✐ NOTES

A Year in Reflection

Floodwaters on the Carrigrohane Straight, Cork

NOVEMBER 27TH

'I have come so that you may have life and have it to the full'
~ John's Gospel 10:10

The above line can be a great starter for prayer. The following little prayer is one of many possibilities. Lord, you don't give anything away in half measures but always complete and full. Your offer of life to us is touching and inspiring. Help me to appreciate that you are the greatest source of life and energy in our world today. Help me to live life to the full and in doing so experience your life and blessings in my life. Even when it seems that the floodwaters are closing in on me, help me to realize that you are always closer to me than I can possibly imagine. Thank you for your gentle presence in my life. Amen

NOTES:

 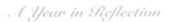

Winter sun through the trees at Tooreenbawn, Millstreet, Co. Cork

NOVEMBER 28TH

There is an old fable in which a mighty oak tree that stood for over one 100 years was finally blown over by a storm. The tree fell into a river and floated downstream until it came to rest among the reeds growing along the riverbank. The fallen giant asked the reeds in amazement: "How is it that you were able to weather the storm that was too powerful for me, an oak tree, to withstand?" The reeds replied, "All these years you stubbornly resisted the winds that swept your way. You took such pride in your strength that you refused to yield, even a little bit. We, on the other hand, have not resisted the winds, but have always bent with them. Life throws much at us and much of it outside our control. It's nearly an impossible task to try and stand up to battle everything that comes our way. Like the reeds, we can let much of what's outside our control blow through us and not uproot us.

 NOTES

A cat enjoying some November sunshine

NOVEMBER 29TH

'As I grow to understand life less and less, I learn to love it more and more.'
~Jules Renard

As we grow older we get a greater sense of the unpredictability of life. We can never say for sure what's around the corner. In fact we're often caught unawares. But life can also be so uplifting, rewarding and colourful. Thankfully these often outweigh the unpredictability of life. We may not understand life or God fully but there is a sense of being met more than halfway. Those who try to understand life or God fully are going to be disappointed. Life is there to be lived, to be enjoyed and to be appreciated. Today may not be our best day, but there are enough good things in it to make up for what's not going well.

NOTES:

A fence leads us into the beautiful Myross Wood Retreat House, Leap, West Cork

NOVEMBER 30TH

'The same fence that shuts others out shuts you in.'
~Bill Copeland

Fencing is very important in keeping boundaries, whether it is in our gardens or fields. It comes in all shapes and sizes in trying to keep people or animals in or out. We too have fences in our lives which set important boundaries. But sometimes we need to take down fences that should have been pulled down or removed a long time ago. For some reason we deliberately keep certain people out of our lives. It might have been some silly argument or some disagreement but life moves on and so should we. Too many fences clutter and restrict. In our gospels Jesus talked much about freedom and how we place too many restrictions on ourselves and others. Can I get rid of unnecessary fences in my life? Can I be as free as God wants me to be?

 NOTES

A Year in Reflection

DECEMBER

December Evening: A sunset casts beautiful colour over Millstreet, Co. Cork

DECEMBER 1ST

There is a story told about a king who had two artists working in his kingdom. As time went on he felt one would be more than enough. To decide which artist would stay he asked them to paint a scene that picked up on peace and tranquility. After a few weeks both artists returned with their work. The first artist had painted a beautiful lake, without even a ripple, surrounded by a beautiful meadow filled with flowers. The king was very impressed. He could feel the peace and calm in the painting. He asked the second artist for his work. This artist showed a waterfall scene and you could feel the power of the water. The king dismissed the painting at once, until the artist asked him to look closer. Near the roaring waterfall were some reeds, with a nest and a bird sitting on the eggs. The king was overwhelmed that beside a roaring waterfall, the bird could find such a peaceful spot and gave this artist the overall prize. In the clutter and busyness of our lives, we too can find peace and calm. We ask God to bring peace and calm into those parts of our lives that are in upheaval at the moment.

Notes:

Magic In The Woods: A feather nestles on a tiny plant in Myross Wood, Leap, West Cork

DECEMBER 2ND

'Life moves pretty fast. If you don't stop to look around once in a while you could miss it.'
~From the movie Ferris Bueller's Day Off

Life certainly moves fast and particularly the next few weeks with the run in to Christmas. Everyone seems to be rushing, time seems to be going faster and the list of things to get done grows longer. But unless we step aside from all of this and literally stop to see where we fit into the bigger picture, we have failed ourselves. That's why the season of Advent provides us with that opportunity to step aside. The sheer speed of life today can literally choke and block out those beautiful, simple and ordinary moments that no money can buy. Advent gives us the chance to appreciate that we are indeed on a privileged journey.

 NOTES

December Colour: A Contoneaster plant is covered in red berries at Tooreenbawn, Millstreet, Co. Cork

DECEMBER 3RD

'No answer is also an answer.'
~Danish Proverb

It's often the case that we look for answers and simply don't find them. This is also the case with prayer. We may feel God hasn't heard because our prayers aren't answered. But God always hears and sometimes the best answer is no answer. Perhaps there is something we need to learn, something that may not be for our good in the long term. God simply wants the best for each of us. We need to realise that sometimes what I want may not necessarily be right just now.

Everything has its own place and time. Somewhere in the middle of all of it are God's plans for me. Few of us can fully understand life as it unfolds. Part of the message of Advent is to put our trust in God even when we're unsure and uncertain of what's going on in our lives.

 NOTES:

Ploughing Forward: The sheer strength of Maxi (Dalmation) and Mandy (Labrador) carry them through the Aubane river near Millstreet, Co. Cork

DECEMBER 4TH

'God doesn't owe us anything but we owe God everything.'
~Colleen Rainone.

We sometimes say "I owe you one", when someone does us a big favour. We appreciate what they've done for us and we want to give something back. We sometimes mistakenly think that if we do everything by the book, that God owes it to us to make things go our way. God really doesn't owe us anything because whatever we do we are loved truly and uniquely by God. It is we who owe God so much, particularly for blessings received. There are times when our shortest prayer to God is, "I owe you one." Hopefully as we edge closer to Christmas, it will also be our prayer, no matter how small or big.

NOTES

A Year in Reflection

'Towering Waves' at Clogher beach on the Dingle Peninsula, Co. Kerry

DECEMBER 5TH

'I give you a new commandment, love one another just as I have loved you.
You must also love one another.
~*John 13:33-34*

Teilard de Chardin once said "Some day, after mastering the winds, the waves, the tides and gravity, we shall harness for God the great energies of love and then for the second time in the history of the world, we will have discovered fire". Love is indeed a powerful force but we can also miss out on all that love has to offer because we are simply too busy. Love is too precious to ignore especially God's love. It is the greatest thing that God can give us and it is also the greatest thing that we can give God. Perhaps Mother Teresa sums it up best. An American journalist was watching Mother Teresa as she cared for a man with gangrene. He said "I wouldn't do that for a million dollars." She replied, "Even I wouldn't do it for that amount! However I do it out of love for God."

NOTES:

Balancing Act: The Harlem Globetrotters give a demonstration of how it's done at Madison Gardens Arena, New York, U.S.

DECEMBER 6TH

'You can't see grass or flowers growing by watching them with the physical eye, but yet they are still growing.'
~Michael Drumm

There are many things in life that are growing and flourishing. It's true that we often don't immediately see all the good and positive around us. Yet it's there in abundance. Some people may be pessimistic, critical and negative and they often make sure that they are heard! God always has a different perspective. Even though everything in life isn't always clear there is much happening. There is much growth and life around. We may not think we're making progress but from God's point of view we're doing really well. We can't see grass growing yet it's happening at its own pace. This can be enough of an incentive to trust all that God has planned for us.

 NOTES

A robin perches and poses for a photo at Fota Gardens, near Cobh, Co. Cork

DECEMBER 7TH

'A bird does not sing because it has an answer, it sings because it has a song.'
~Chinese Proverb

Unfortunately we don't have all the answers to everything in life or never will. Many waste a lot of energy trying to find those answers. Each of us, despite not having all the answers, has so much to give. Our song, our personality, our gifts and talents and all we have to offer make us uniquely special. Many of our songs lie dormant and unused and this is a great shame. As we journey through Advent the invitation is to bring to life those areas that may be lying dormant. We pray for the courage to believe in our abilities and in what we have to offer. Today I can be proud of my song and especially proud of who I am.

NOTES:

A Year in Reflection

A Unique Moment: Some pictures say it all. This one needs no explaining except to say that it's Daniel McSweeney making the most of life in hospital.

DECEMBER 8TH

'The foundations for a better tomorrow must be laid today.'
~Author Unknown

There are many building sites across the city and county at the moment. Some are at the early stages with big deep foundations being laid. The best of houses, apartments and buildings will fade into insignificance unless there is a rock solid foundation underneath. Today is the feast of the Immaculate Conception of Mary. Traditionally it begins the official countdown to Christmas. Mary was marked out by God to play a hugely significant role as the mother of Jesus. She was a rock solid foundation in everything she did. Mary was not removed or shielded from all of life's joys and tribulations. She too experienced everything that we go through. Her feast day today reminds us of the importance of a good solid foundation in all we do. Like Mary, living today well is a great foundation stone in preparing for tomorrow.

NOTES

A Year in Reflection

Holly branches at Myross Wood Retreat House, Leap, West Cork

DECEMBER 9TH

'Don't walk in front of me I may not follow. Don't walk behind me I may not lead.
Walk beside be and just be my friend.
~Author Unknown

There are high expectations put on all of us in these weeks before Christmas. Some of these are artificially high. We're expected to be in good form, to be in good spirits, to be able to buy gifts at ease and to be in many places at one time. Not everyone can meet these high expectations and this can lead to so much unnecessary stress and worry. The greatest gift we can give to those closest to us is to walk with them and be their friend. When we do this we pull down all expectations and allow someone just to be themselves. No shopping catalogue could ever match such a gift.

 NOTES:

Keeping Watch: A fantail dove perches up on a lantern at the live animal Christmas Crib at Kilmorna Heights, Ballyvolane, Cork

DECEMBER 10TH

'We are not restful persons who occasionally get restless but rather restless persons who occasionally find rest.'
~Henri Nouwen

Our world today is restless; so are we. We're looking for what will bring us contentment, peace and a sense of being happy with what we're doing. There are many things to buy, so many things to do and so many options with travel. But these don't satisfy our deepest longings. We search and long for a soul mate, some person who understands us through and through, someone who loves us to bits. Perhaps you are one of the lucky ones who has already found it, or you may have found it but it didn't work out or you may still be searching. No wait can take from God who is our ultimate soul mate with whom we are always at home with. The sometimes shallow and hectic pace of life can never compensate for the times when we find true rest with someone special or with God.

NOTES

A light snow shower covers fir trees on the lower slopes of Mushera mountain near Millstreet, Co. Cork

DECEMBER 11TH

'It is said that sheep may get lost simply by nibbling away at grass and never looking up. That can be true for any of us. We can focus so much on what is immediately before us that we fail to see life in larger perspective.'
~Donald Bitsberger

With everyone living hectic lives just before Christmas, the chances are high that we could end up like those sheep. We're all aware of just so much to do. Trying to squeeze everything in can leave us exhausted. What we do and hope to do is of course important but not if we forget to keep everything in perspective. Keeping the bigger picture in mind is indeed important. The very fact that 80% of the world's population live in some form of poverty is always a great starter in keeping our feet on the ground. This Christmas will provide many opportunities to be grateful to God for the smallest of deeds and gestures done out of love and kindness. I can't do everything but I can do so much more when I begin to prioritise what's important and avoid what's shallow and empty.

NOTES:

Crazy: A driver tries to brave it through the floods, only to get caught further up along the Carrigrohane Straight, Cork

DECEMBER 12TH

'Nobody trips over mountains. It is the small pebble that causes us to stumble. Pass all the pebbles in your path and you will find that you have crossed the mountain.'
~Author Unknown

We all go through obstacles or walls on our daily journey. Some we see coming and some are unexpected. Some are challenging and difficult, while more are easy to cross. But each one needs to be faced with determination and courage. The day we become complacent and careless is indeed the day that we will stumble and fall. During these hectic few weeks before Christmas it is surprising what causes us to stumble. It is often the many small things together which can cause us to stumble. These days of Advent remind us that no obstacle, flood, or barrier can come between us and God's personal love for us. It is easy to become complacent but Advent keeps our feet firmly on the ground.

 NOTES

A hen nestles in to lay an egg in the live animal Christmas crib at Kilmorna Heights, Ballyvolane

DECEMBER 13TH

Little Johnny was a holy terror all day. He seized every moment to be up to mischief. His exasperated mother was reaching the end of her patience. She had tried everything to get him to be good. As a final resort she asked him to pray to God to be good. To her surprise, he sat down with his hands joined in prayer. This went on for a few minutes and then he rose looking remarkably repentant. "Well John, did God say you were to be a good boy?" asked his mum. "Yes" said John, "but that it might take a little longer than expected!"

Our patience is often tested. We know what we want but it just doesn't seem to be happening. A Chinese proverb sums it up well by saying if we are patient in one moment of trial, we will escape a hundred days of sorrow. We ask God to help us to be patient, to trust that the tide will turn and to know that God is always on our side.

NOTES:

Our Resting Place: These boats rest easy on a calm December evening at Ballylickey, West Cork

December 14th

*'I believe in the light even when the sun doesn't shine. I believe in love even when it isn't given. I believe in God even when God's voice is silent.' **~Author unknown** - but was found scratched on the wall of an air raid shelter in Germany after the World War II*

We can all relate to moments when the sun doesn't shine in our lives, when life doesn't seem to be going our way and even when God seems to be silent in our lives. The only consolation is that such moments aren't just confined to us but are experienced by many people. It takes great courage and faith to keep believing when all seems against us. But this is what we are called to do. The effort will pay dividends because somewhere along the line the light does and will break through. God's voice may be silent but God continues to journey with us. That quiet voice will become audible.

 NOTES

Falling in Love!: at the live animal Christmas crib, Kilmorna Heights, Ballyvolane

DECEMBER 15TH

There is a well known story about a basketball coach in New York who had the rare art of inspiring teams with the courage to fight back when things looked impossible. During the half-time at one difficult game he stood before the team and yelled, "Did John F Kennedy ever quit?" The team roared back "No!" "Did the Wright brothers ever quit" The team yelled "No!" "Did Neil Armstrong or Michael Jordan ever quit" Again the answer "No" was yelled back. "Did John McAllister ever quit?" asked the coach looking around at the whole team. There was an awkward pause. Then the team captain said "coach, we never heard of him." "Of course you didn't", shouted the coach. "He quit!"

The prophet Isaiah has an equally impressive line, "Tell everyone who is discouraged to be strong and not to be afraid. God is coming to your rescue." At our deepest moment of discouragement we are called to dig in deep, to trust in God and not to quit when it's tempting to do so.

 NOTES:

Christmas Smiles: Mary Nolan with Conor enjoying a lighter moment at the live animal Christmas crib, Ballyvolane

DECEMBER 16TH

'Remember, if Christmas isn't found in your heart, you won't find it under the tree.'
~Charlotte Carpenter

Christmas can mean many different things to many people. We all strive for peace, harmony, direction and stability in life. Few achieve this fully in their lifetime but we can certainly go a long way towards it. Christmas is always a great starting point but only a starting point. Too often we expect too much and high expectations always lead to disappointment. No one is going to wave a magic wand and tell us that life or this Christmas is going to be perfect. But it can certainly be a great starting point towards peace, harmony, direction and stability in my life.

 NOTES

Getting Ready: Some of Santa's deer get ready for their long journey in a week's time.

DECEMBER 17TH

'In healing one can concentrate on either of two attributes, the power of God or the love of God. But in every healing there is a manifestation of both.'
~Francis MacNutt

There is a part of everyone's life that needs healing. It isn't just confined to health but it can be any part of our lives that needs the gentle touch of God. Medicine is one of God's gifts to initiate and sustain healing but all the prescriptions in the world cannot compete with deep spiritual healing. If we are not open to healing itself, it will struggle to happen in our lives. Our prayer today as we move closer to Christmas is to pray for God's gentle healing and gentle touch in our lives. We ask for this especially in those areas of our lives that are vulnerable and exposed, those parts of our lives that need closure. With every healing is the promise of new life and new beginnings especially this Christmas.

NOTES:

Crib Reflections: at the Lough, Cork

DECEMBER 18TH

'The most exhausting thing in life is being insincere.'
~Anne Lindberg

A story is told about St. Francis walking towards a town with a fellow friar. Just before they enter, Francis turns to his companion and tells him he plans on preaching the gospel there. As they walk through, Francis laughs and plays with the children, comforts someone ill on the side of the road and prays with an elderly man who had just lost his wife. As they are leaving, the companion of Francis looks at him and says, "I thought you were going to preach the gospel." Francis turned to him and said "I just did." So often we put our expectations of God on a pedestal. We expect something out of the ordinary, when in fact God is really present in the ordinary, down to earth events of our own lives. Like St. Francis we can experience God closer to us than we can possibly imagine.

NOTES

Collection Time: Fresh eggs all ready to go in the live animal Christmas crib, Ballyvolane

December 19th

'Noise proves nothing. Often a hen who has merely laid an egg
cackles as if she had laid an asteroid.'
~Mark Twain

Coming from a farming background myself this is probably a little harsh on the hen. True, they do tend to make a lot of noise sometimes when they lay an egg, but often she is simply happy and proud of what she has done. We live in a noisy world and we have grown used to more and more noise around us. Such noise is now seen as normal. Unfortunately it destroys any sense of silence, peace and quietness which the human soul craves for. Noise is a part of our daily lives but we also need to check in on the noise levels of our own lives. What are the noise levels around me as I read this? Can I sit quietly even for a few minutes and thank the Lord for the quiet time. It is one of the best gifts we can give to ourselves any day

NOTES:

Liam McElhinney delivers a huge cuddly toy after the proceeds of a Christmas Toy Mass at St. Oliver's Church, Ballyvolane

DECEMBER 20TH

'When we fill a vessel drop by drop, there is at last one drop which will make it run over. So it is with a series of kindnesses, there is at last one which makes the heart run over.'
~James Boswell

Every single act of kindness never goes to waste. Sometimes we do something good and think it won't make a difference or will be noticed. The simple fact is that every act of kindness makes a real and lasting difference in someone's life. Here in Cork many young people will be collecting on the streets of Cork for Share right up to Christmas Eve. It is a proud part of Cork's tradition. Every little given to Share will make a huge difference in someone's life. We should never underestimate the difference a little kindness can make in someone's life this Christmas. Only we can initiate it and make it happen. As the old saying goes, 'every little helps.'

NOTES

Beam of Hope: A beam of sunlight runs along Ballintotis Lake, near Castlemartyr, Co. Cork

DECEMBER 21ST

'I believe in Christianity as I believe that the sun has risen. I do so not only because I see it but because by it, I can see everything else.'
~C.S Lewis

The Winter Solstice marks a crucial part of the natural cycle. In a real sense, the sun begins anew its journey towards longer days, times of new growth and a renewal of the world once again. In a spiritual sense, it is a reminder that in order for a new path to begin, the old one must come to an end. This Christmas can also be the end of old and worn roads in my life. Instead there is the opportunity to walk new and fresh roads, roads that are life giving and meaningful. Daylight may be scarce today but God's light and love are to be found in abundance particularly as we edge ever so close to Christmas.

NOTES:

A full moon at Christmas comes up through a forest at Tooreenbawn, Millstreet, Co. Cork

DECEMBER 22ND

'Anyone who has really understood that God became human can
never speak and act in an inhuman way.'
~Karl Barth

Christmas is indeed celebrated in so many different ways. Tradition is always a winner in this last week before Christmas. It might be making plans to pick up the turkey, going out with friends, sending off those last few Christmas cards, looking forward to welcoming home extended family or squeezing in some final shopping. All our plans are shallow unless we first have a sense of what Christmas is all about. The significance of God coming into this world to be one like us could easily be lost. In becoming one like us God wants to come ever so close to us. God knows what's going on for each of us, our joys and struggles, our weak and strong points, our disappointments and plans. To really understand how close God is to us can be and is life changing.

NOTES

Rudolf is all ready to go tomorrow night!

December 23rd

'We understand why children are afraid of darkness but why are people afraid of light?'
~Plato

Everyone lives in some shadow or darkness in life. It is hard to avoid difficulties and circumstances that don't go our way. They often come to us unexpectedly and at a time we least expect. But we don't have to live in these shadows forever. The message of Christmas is all about light and a call towards light, hope and new beginnings in our own lives. We can be afraid of many things but there are no grounds to be afraid of God's light. The many Christmas lights on display are doing their best to brighten up our dark winter evenings. But only God's light can penetrate the darkest of corners. This Christmas the invitation is to be open to God's light, whether it's a little chink or a big beam. It's not about how much or how little, but all about being open to it.

 Notes:

Ssshhh! I'm on my way and I hope you've been good!

DECEMBER 24TH

'There are those who are so scrupulously afraid of doing wrong that they seldom venture to do anything.'
~Author Unknown

Everyone strides to give and do their best each day. It is what God asks of each of us. Sometimes we do get it wrong and most times we get it just about right. But getting it wrong is not so earth shattering that we can't pick up the pieces and learn from where we went wrong. On this Christmas Eve it's good to know that now is an ideal time to begin to pick up those pieces and move forward with our lives. Christmas is not about getting it just perfect, cosy and right. A humble stable on the side of a hill was far from perfect. It is much more about doing my best in all my struggles and in what works best for me. That's where God is most active in my life. No one can take that from me anytime.

NOTES

The crib in St. Oliver's Church, Ballyvolane, sums up what today is all about.

December 25th

'I am not alone as I thought I was. I am never alone at all.
And that, of course, is the message of Christmas. We are never alone. Not when the night is darkest, the wind coldest, the world seemingly most indifferent.
For this is still the time God chooses.'
~Taylor Caldwell

God will always choose the moment we do not expect. Just as we thought the stable was not the ideal place for a baby to be born so it is with our own lives. God chooses to be a part of our lives when we least expect it. Everyone who came to the first crib was welcome. The same goes with all of us this Christmas. No matter what our story, background or situation, we are all welcome at God's crib. There are no barriers and no exceptions. Everyone is welcome and we are never alone. Wishing you a happy, holy and peaceful Christmas.

 Notes:

A White Christmas: The sunlight breaks through the snow covered branches near Berrings, Co. Cork

DECEMBER 26TH

'Let those who never loved before love now. Let those who always loved, love a little more.'
~Author Unknown

Hopefully your Christmas went well for you. Perhaps today St. Stephen's Day, there is a sense of relief that it's all over and looking forward now to the New Year. Even though Christmas stretches to twelve days we will now be replacing 'Happy Christmas' with 'Happy New Year!' But one thing about Christmas is that its real message should never be lost. The invitation is to carry it with us every single day. The real message of Christmas evolves around love. It is the energy that brings meaning and life to all we do. We can begin to find God's love again in our lives and to share it with others no matter how small. These days are indeed sacred and special. It is up to us to make the most of them in whatever way we can.

 NOTES

A Year in Reflection 361

Christmas at Tooreenbawn, Millstreet, Co. Cork

DECEMBER 27TH

'There's none so blind as those who will not see.'
~Old Proverb

Many people have been credited with a quick eye and who miss absolutely nothing. However, in matters of general observation we do tend to leave out a lot. We think all greens are green until we take a walk out into the countryside. A simple Christmas candle in a Church or home can speak volumes about hope, light and life. With the build up to Christmas we may have been so busy and hectic that we could have our eyes closed to what's really important. What's really important can often happen in a moment and may never repeat itself again. This week after Christmas is a week to really unwind, relax and take it easy. We ask God to help us make the most of what's precious and special in the closing days of this year.

NOTES:

Rowing in Harmony: Making the most of a sunny morning along the River Lee, near Blackrock Castle, Cork

DECEMBER 28TH

'Don't be envious if the grass is greener on the other side of the fence. It's also harder to cut.'
~Author Unknown

It's often we look at the other side of the fence. We look at people's lifestyles, looks, fashion, and houses. Everything on the other side of the fence seems so attractive. It appears that other people have it so good. But the reality is that these people are looking over the fence too and wishing for what we have. What appears as the perfect lifestyle by someone else is often far from perfect. Our humble patch is where we will find all we need for fulfilment and progress. As we move closer towards a new year our humble patch may need clearing out. Once that's done we can begin to look forward to new beginnings. God always encourages us to work with what we have and not with what others have. It's a great formula for greener grass, on our side.

NOTES

An orange skyline highlights the melting snow on the hills near Rylane, Co. Cork

DECEMBER 29TH

'Doing the best at this moment puts us in the best place for the next moment.'
~Oprah Winfrey

The strings of a guitar on their own are important. They are separate, different and unique. When they choose to come together they can make great sounds. It is the same with moments. Each day is made up of many moments and the vast majority of them are good and positive. God calls us to do our best with each moment that comes our way. This puts us in the best place for the next moment. All our moments put together can make for great sounds. This year is nearly out but there are still moments left to make them memorable and precious. These moments make today worthwhile and keeps us in touch with what's important and life giving.

NOTES:

Bravehearts: Motocross riders showing how it's done at Vernon Mount, Cork

DECEMBER 30TH

'Our task is to seek and find Christ in our world as it is and not as it might be.'
~Thomas Merton

The Pieta by Michelangelo is one of the world's most famous sculptures. It is of Mary holding the body of Jesus at the foot of the cross and is so lifelike that one can almost feel the heartbreak of a mother holding her lifeless son. Back in 1972 a man with a hammer jumped the railing and smashed the statue fifteen times with a hammer. It broke into over fifty big pieces and countless more tiny pieces. Sympathy, advice and money poured into the Vatican from all over the world. Many doubted it could be repaired but for the next year a team worked on putting it all back piece by piece. A year later it was unveiled and looked as it was except for a scar that they left on the veil of Mary to remind people of what happened and that nothing in this world is perfect, even the Pieta.

 NOTES

Pushing Forth: As we say goodbye to one year and look forward to a new one, daffodils are already pushing through at Tooreenbawn, Millstreet, Co. Cork

DECEMBER 31ST

'The flower does not bear the root. The root bears the flower and the flower is merely the evidence of the vitality of the root.'
~ Woodview Wilson

We are about to say goodbye to the year just gone. There are parts of the year just gone, that we're glad to leave behind. It may have been a personal tragedy, bereavement, an illness, family troubles, mistakes made and much more. For some the new year just cannot come soon enough. But there are also parts of this year that were special, influential and memorable. These moments are worth remembering and holding on to. Like the roots of a plant or tree they are vitally important. They can give us direction and sustenance as we begin a new year. We say thanks for God's gentle presence in our lives throughout the year just gone. This includes both what was good and not so good. God's continued blessings on you as we begin a new year

 NOTES: